90 Days
to Launch

90 Days
to Launch

INTERNET PROJECTS
ON TIME AND ON BUDGET

Shayne F. Gilbert

JOHN WILEY & SONS, INC.

New York • Chichester • Weinheim • Brisbane • Singapore • Toronto

Published by John Wiley & Sons, Inc.
Published simultaneously in Canada.

This publication is designed to provide accurate and authoritative information in regard to the subject matter covered. It is sold with the understanding that the publisher is not engaged in rendering legal, accounting, or other professional services. If legal advice or other expert assistance is required, the services of a competent professional person should be sought.

Library of Congress Cataloging-in-Publication Data:

Gilbert, Shayne, 1966–
    90 days to launch : Internet projects on time and on budget / by Shayne Gilbert.
        p.   cm.
    Includes bibliographical references and index.
    ISBN 0-471-38826-2 (cloth : alk. paper)
    1. Internet. 2. Websites. 3. Industrial project management. I. Title.
    HD30.37 .G55   2000
    658.8'4—dc21

                                                                                00-042269

Printed in the United States of America.

10 9 8 7 6 5 4 3 2 1

To the people who launched me,
my parents, Dianne and Henry

Preface

Have you ever flown into a city where you've never been, put the keys into the ignition of the rental car, driven out the gate, stopped at the first crossroad, and, with a heavy sinking feeling, realized that you have no idea how to get to your meeting? Today, launching a web site on time and on budget is like sitting at that crossroad—you know where you want to be, but you have no directions to get there. *90 Days to Launch* gives you those directions. By following the step-by-step instructions outlined in this book, you will develop the directions or guidelines that will enable your company to launch a site on time and on budget. Over the past six years, I have worked with well-established companies like Lucent and BankBoston, as well as with fast-growth Internet start-ups like Etrav.com and Zoots.com, to implement these guidelines. Although the resources may be varied, the end results are consistent—launching a site on time and on budget.

The first step in launching a site on time and on budget is to define the business objectives and clearly set realistic milestones. Sure, everyone wants to receive millions of hits (or impressions, or unique visitors) on his or her site. But how many people know how many customers they can acquire through these hits before their back-office systems overload and they can't service the needs of all those new customers? Sony has developed a great direct-to-customer site for the sale of its computer notebooks but still can't deliver the products if they're not in inventory. At the same time, PC Connection online, because of its inventory allotment, may have a greater supply on hand. Does Sony choke its distribution channel in an effort to beef up its own direct-to-end-user inventory? Levi's, after approximately a year of selling direct to consumer through their web site, actually took the strategy offline in what is believed to be a response to channel conflict. As detailed in the first few chapters, the first step in developing the project guidelines is to set realistic business objectives.

Having achieved consensus at the corporate level, the next step is to assess the market conditions by defining the constituents, assessing the competitive marketplace, developing a differentiable customer relationship strategy, and merging the existing systems into the online marketplace. Focusing on the constituents, is the goal customer acquisition or customer retention? If the goal is customer service, then a primary constituent may be the internal customer service staff. Lands' End uses "LivePerson" technology to give its customers immediate online access to a customer service representative. Not only does this service differentiate Lands' End's relationship with customers from that of its competitors but it also deepens the ongoing relationship for future sales. However, for each "LivePerson" exchange, there are two constituents involved: (1) a customer and (2) a service representative. Furthermore, service systems must be retrofitted to deftly respond to this new customer management process.

Once the business objectives and market conditions have been approved, the third step is to define the resources.

These resources include creating the technical blueprint for the system architecture (including hardware, applications, system integration, and custom development), assembling the vendor team, and creating the project schedule. These components become part of the request for proposal (RFP). With realistic business objectives and a project plan defined by these guidelines, a site can be launched in 90 days, but it will require tight objectives that can respond and scale rapidly. Hotmail, the free e-mail service, responded to a direct market need—the demand for private e-mail. Because every e-mail was branded "hotmail," customers became salespeople, rapidly spreading the word and creating new customers.

Finally, with guidelines well defined, rapid web site development can begin. Thus, the final step in developing the rapid launch guidelines is the project plan. Like a good roadmap, with a well-developed project plan, a web site can be launched on time and on budget.

SHAYNE F. GILBERT

Acknowledgments

In 2000, building a successful online strategy requires ingenuity. In 1994, creating a consulting practice around the delivery of effective online strategies required tremendous vision. *90 Days to Launch* would not have been possible without the vision of the many people who were willing to take a chance and to work with me as I built a consulting practice around the Internet economy. Robert Levine, Beth Ginsberg, Steven Peck, Sally Jackson, Jerome Sohn, Richard Van Pelt, Jeff Shuman, and Jeanie-Marie Price provided invaluable wisdom and support in building the practice.

Heartfelt appreciation to those peers, colleagues, and clients who took the time to critique the early stages of the book, including Mark Prahl, Stuart Hilger, Gary Frawley, Margy Stratton Norman, Michael Eizenberg, Nicole Wilkerson, Frank Selldorff, Michael Borum, and Lee Levitt. I would also like to thank all of my clients and students.

Thanks also to my early mentors, Chip Case and Byrne Murphy, who were both patient and understanding as they taught me the fundamentals of smart economics and business practices.

I am also tremendously grateful to Doris Michaels, my agent, who first recognized the potential, and to the entire editorial team at Wiley who created the market opportunity for *90 Days to Launch*.

Finally, I would like to thank those close friends and family who have given me the strength, courage, and inspiration to pursue my own dreams. To Faye and George, for their love and support. To my grandfather, Martin, whose unique combination of love and wisdom has always been a source of inspiration. To my siblings, Barry, Alyssa, and Susan, for their unwavering belief and encouragement. And, finally, once again, to my parents, Dianne and Henry, whose steadfast belief that I could do anything that I set out to accomplish enabled me to be the person that I am today.

S.F.G.

Contents

Part I
Definition of Business Objectives

Chapter 1

Defining the Project
Management Path

For decades, success was the product of the steady yet sometimes slow implementation of tried-and-true strategies. Inheriting a corporate title meant that there were already processes in place for certain business functions. There was a certain level of inherited business strategy built into product-driven positions, such as brand manager, marketing director, and vice president of product development—until the Internet. All of a sudden, new business rules were being written and then rewritten before the ink could dry; and with these new rules came new career opportunities: director of online strategies, new media manager, and vice president of Internet initiatives. All of these new positions have one common goal: to deliver a sustainable online strategy, on time and on budget. For those managers who have chosen to define and to shape evolving business standards, *90 Days to Launch* offers a practical guide to delivering a web strategy and to going live with the site on time and on budget. In the hyper-accelerated pace of the Internet, 90 days—a single business quarter—can define a market leader as rapidly as it can

3

condemn a market dinosaur. Because the successful market strategies are often rewarded by the public markets, quarterly financial reports are often the benchmarks that drive the 90-day launch of the web site.

■ THE ONLINE STRATEGY

The primary step in creating a strategy that can be delivered in 90 days is first to target the business area in need of upgrading and then to define the Internet solution. For example, the traditional cost to stock a large inventory of goods limits the choices that a business can offer its customers. If the customer can select the products while they are still in the warehouse, the distribution costs are significantly diminished. With customer access to inventory, products can then be stored in a centralized facility and shipped overnight. A web site can provide that access, both increasing customer choice and decreasing distribution-carrying costs. For example, the strategy behind Webvan is to create a centralized facility for groceries and other consumer goods. By housing the inventory in a centralized facility, Webvan saves the cost of maintaining, stocking, and distributing goods through retail stores. At the same time, consumers, through the Webvan site, are given access to a wider variety of goods that are then conveniently delivered to the home.

With a focused online strategy, the Internet becomes a vehicle to solve traditional operational problems. *Indirect access* to customer demand creates a problem for manufacturers who want to develop tighter inventory controls. If a manufacturer could communicate directly with the customer, products could be manufactured more in line with current rather than anticipated customer demand. Just-in-time data delivers a solution. Through a web site, customers all over the world can inexpensively communicate their needs directly to the manufacturer. The major automobile manufacturers are moving in this direction with consumer-focused web sites that enable the end user to preview and to specify options prior to auto purchase. This strategy, in turn, drives manufacturing efficiencies because products are delivered to customer specification rather than to customer speculation.

Proximity to the client adds to the challenge of managing projects. Responsiveness is bound by the time constraints of planning, scheduling, and completing a meeting. The cost of planning a meeting, synchronizing schedules, concisely delivering the service, and anticipating returns is inefficient and costly. Through a web site, projects can be delivered through a collaborative solution. The ability to collaborate online—an efficiency traditionally enabled only through complex Internet solutions—is rapidly emerging as a major Internet benefit. Servers that traditionally housed web-based files are now being reconfigured through companies like X-Collaboration as a way to seamlessly share documents and jointly manage information via the Internet. In the legal community, the ability to house and to distribute secure documents for review by multiple parties will streamline and offer new efficiencies in the traditionally document-laden legal process.

Low switching costs for consumers impacts a company's ability to sustain its market share. With identical products stacking brick-and-mortar shelves, consumers may be driven into a store by brand but commit to a product by price. On the web, the purchase of a product can be more efficiently tracked and managed. For example, the online store developed by Hewlett-Packard was created to support the ongoing service needs of the customer after the purchase. When a customer purchases a replacement cartridge for a specific printer at the online store, this information is stored internally to facilitate future purchases. Over time, this new approach to customer service online, in which consumer loyalty is emphasized through follow-on support and service, deepens customer relationships and diminishes the traditionally low switching costs of retail acquisition.

Supply chain delays have always been crisis points for traditional companies, but with the Internet, roles in the supply chain have blurred. The U.S. government, by using the Internet to solicit for supplies, has opened up supply chain channels to vendors who did not have access to the traditional paperbound solicitation process. Increasing access to additional suppliers creates a more competitive bidding opportunity. Simultaneously, by centralizing solicitation through an extranet solution, the potential buying power increases among individual businesses who can form coalitions to respond to specific requests.

Despite the hype, the Internet is not a panacea for the myriad of dilemmas that a company faces each day. However, with well-executed planning, development, and execution of Internet solutions, the Internet can deliver immediate, significant benefits to traditional business processes.

Through the methodology carefully outlined, *90 Days to Launch* illustrates how to develop a high-level strategic plan that addresses the overall business issues and corporate goals for the web site:

➤ Step one, *definition of business objectives,* defines the framework for setting realistic business objectives and achievable corporate results. After senior-level approval of the strategic plan, the process can move to step two.

➤ Step two, *assessment of market conditions,* reviews the process to define the target market and user base, assess the competition, deliver a competitive marketing strategy, and formalize the online positioning strategy.

➤ Step three, *identification of resources,* describes how to assess both the internal and external skills and resources necessary to deliver the strategic plan. Critical to this step is a well-defined description of the project requirements, or blueprint, which can then be used as the baseline for a request for proposal (RFP) to outside vendors. A customizable version of the blueprint is located online at the *90 Days to Launch* web site—www.90daystolaunch.com. Here, readers can download a copy of the blueprint to adapt to their own web site vendor solicitations; they can also share strategies and insights with other Internet managers.

➤ Step four, *implementation,* is the actual development, delivery, and ongoing management of the guidelines as outlined.

BLUEPRINT

The RFP is the vendor version of the project blueprint that defines the specific details that will enable the on time on budget launch.

■ STEP ONE: DEFINITION OF BUSINESS OBJECTIVES

Before an achievable Internet plan can be delivered, management must make some non-Internet business decisions that will establish the project's overall business objectives. Whether this is to launch a new product line or to increase customer support, these decisions will set the criteria by which the web site strategy will be implemented. Once that decision is approved, then the development of the web site project plan can begin.

In this stage, the Internet plan is a high-level strategy. At its core is the web site strategic statement. This statement reflects the constraints of traditional business processes, states the objective of the online strategy, and succinctly notes the quantifiable results to be achieved by the online strategy. It consists primarily of two sections: (1) a substantiated review of the traditional business process and any of its shortcomings and (2) a projected view of the online business process. The strategic plan begins with a simple statement of the web site objective. As outlined in the following example, this objective should capture both the short-term need and the long-term result. For example, one web site strategy may be to turn one-time customers into lifetime customers or, succinctly stated:

The web site will create lifetime customers.

That statement is a very noble ambition, but it does not address how it will happen or what the measurable results are. The next step is to meet with the marketing and sales departments to learn more about the history of the company's relationships with its customers: How does the company traditionally acquire customers? How many of these customers become repeat buyers? Why do customers leave? Only after understanding these traditional fundamentals can a focused online strategy be achieved.

Through this internal due diligence, the Internet manager may discover that although traditional advertising strategies may produce a high level of awareness among potential customers, only half of those customers become regular repeat purchasers. And the reason that customers do not purchase the product again is because, when purchasing in a retail store, they are presented with less expensive products that claim to deliver the same benefit. From a lifetime relationship perspective, the goal thus becomes twofold:

1. Educate the customer about the differentiated product benefits.
2. Provide a sales channel in which the competition does not exist.

Now the web site's objective becomes more directed:

To create lifetime customers, the web site will demonstrate product benefits and will create a direct sales channel.

However, the targeted results for this initiative have still not been defined. For example, are 1,000 random visits an adequate measure of a successful Internet strategy? What if there are 1,000 prospective customer visits in six months? Three months? Two weeks? The term *prospective customer* also has to be predefined. Is a prospective customer someone who simply visits the site or someone who provides their e-mail address in exchange for additional information? Remember that the development and administration of the web site will shift resources from other strategies. One thousand new, educated consumers in a six-month time frame may not be a relative value when one considers that traditional marketing strategies may generate 10,000 educated consumers in the same time period. The measurable results (which, of course, will evolve over time) may be to generate 10,000 new visitors per month and to turn 1 percent (100 per month) of these visitors into lifetime customers. Once again, the initial strategic statement is further focused:

To increase the total number of lifetime customers by 1,200 per year, the web site will demonstrate product benefits and will deliver a direct sales channel.

Acquisition of these lifetime customers will most likely be achieved through a combination of both traditional and online marketing strategies. As outlined further in Chapter 6 on branding, promotion of the web site address through all traditional marketing channels will support the online initiative.

The strategic statement of the web site objective therefore must incorporate not only the overall objective of the web site strategy but also definable (and deliverable) action items, as well as quantifiable results. Lack of either will create a web site with noble ambitions but vague results. Step one delivers the guidelines to succinctly define the business objectives of senior management.

■ STEP TWO: ASSESSMENT OF MARKET CONDITIONS

With senior-level approval of the strategic plan, the next step is to consider the market landscape. With the primary constituent base defined in the strategic plan, consideration should also be given to other potential constituents. This may include potential customers who were outside of the traditional marketing strategies and who may be interested because of accessibility through the web.

During this stage, it is critical to define the target audience. Unlike business users, 17-year-olds, when visiting a site, are going to drive through in a staccato click of pages. Conversely, in business, purchase managers are going to methodically window shop, looking for the ultimate best deal. Capture them by educating them, and keep them by creating a single-click purchase process. Better yet, track their purchase needs for them by becoming their virtual inventory system, and keep their shelves permanently stocked for them. HomeRuns.com, a northeast home grocery service, will "remember" previous orders placed through their online system and will create an automatic "personal shopping list" when the customer returns for their next order.

New customers will expect a different experience than repeat customers. Corporate partners, such as resellers, may also visit the site for product information, but they will have different expectations for product details. Investors, current and prospective, will also have a unique set of expectations, while the press will have an entirely different perspective when they visit the site. The first step in developing a successful positioning strategy is to define and to prioritize the target audiences and their anticipated experience.

While the hope is that the majority of visitors will be welcome on the site, the reality is that the site will probably attract unwelcome visitors in the form of competition. Expect this, and take the initiative when positioning the site against the competition. Because the Internet redefines the rules of who may be a competitor, use the search engines to help define the competition. Select key industry terms, and enter them in some of the top search engines. Track the results and visit the sites. Consider, also, that some popular results may not be direct competitors (different customer base, geographic concentration) and could be considered potential partners that can assist in the development of an industry portal, targeting the needs of a specific industry sector, through cross-links and similar promotions. After careful review, create a positioning chart, and track it over time to make sure that the site retains its competitive edge. Plastics-Net creates a consolidated portal for suppliers to sell their goods in the plastics industry. By creating a single resource, PlasticsNet significantly increased the potential reach of individual suppliers.

Finally, after reviewing the competitive marketplace, create an overall positioning strategy. Is there room for a clear market leader, or is it a highly fragmented online community? Is technology advanced throughout the sites,

INTERNET PROJECT PLAN

The Internet project plan or blueprint defines the business requirements that will be delivered through the project implementation. It is a critical component to the launch of a successful site. Written by the project manager, it synthesizes the goals and the objectives of the entire project team. It should typically include six major sections that succinctly define the objectives and the resources of the various team members:

1. *The Strategic Statement*—defines the top-level corporate objectives and reflects the business requirements of senior management.

2. *The Positioning Statement*—reflects the needs of the target audience and defines the competitive environment.

3. *Branding of the Site*—reflecting the established corporate brand, defines the internal design specifications and lays the groundwork for the online user interface.

4. *Choice of Architecture*—developed by the information technology (IT) department, defines legacy systems and existing architectures that will impact the processes to be developed and delivered through the online strategy.

5. *Vendor Requirements*—delivered by the vendors, assesses their core competencies and experiences to ensure they are consistent with the overall objectives.

6. *Timeline and Budget*—generally set by the project manager but fine-tuned by the vendor team. This section defines the specific milestones and individual line items that determine the project schedule and costs.

or is there opportunity for automation that will leave the competition in the dust? The positioning strategy will deliver a focused implementation program for the strategic plan. Step two provides the guidelines to deliver the target audience.

■ STEP THREE: IDENTIFICATION OF RESOURCES

The next step is to create a working document or work plan that will define the project deliverables. This business work plan will serve to define the specific resources to deliver the web site. The end result of this step is an RFP.

With project creep endemic in a rapidly evolving industry, a well-documented blueprint will help ensure a timely and cost-effective launch.

■ STEP FOUR: IMPLEMENTATION

After carefully defining the project resources, the next step is to create a strategy to manage the site after the launch. Once the vendor selection process has been completed, the project blueprint will become the core components of the management plan. It will include an outline of all the project deliverables and detailed specifications of design, technology, and content for the site, as well as the introduction of the ongoing administration and maintenance of the site. The plan should include not only the site development but also the ongoing operational strategy. For example, when the development team turns over the virtual keys to the web site, what happens next? Does the vendor hand over a manual, provide infinite support, and deliver a series of training workshops, or does it wave a long good-bye on the way to the bank?

Training and support should also be addressed as part of the project management plan. There are industry-standard representations and warranties, but they do not necessarily cover such details as updating the site, providing access 24 hours a day, 7 days a week (24/7), or incorporating newer technologies. For example, what will the process be to update the site once it has been launched? Will there be a fleet of young web page editors hired in-house to update the site night and day? Alternatively, will it become the additional responsibility of an administrative team who do not know how to code web pages but who are responsible for creating the content? In the former case, access to the original web files may be adequate. In the latter case, simple-to-edit input screens with a back-end database or the delivery of word processing templates that can be saved and sent to the site may be appropriate. Whatever the solution, if it is not addressed early, it could cost significant dollars in the long term.

The site will require daily administration to meet the underlying business objectives. The Internet manager could continue to drive the strategic vision, but it may be appropriate to assign this day-to-day responsibility of the site to an operational manager, sometimes called the web master or web manager. Like the Internet manager, the operational manager should be a generalist who understands the technical architecture but who also has the ability to maintain the integrity of the site's online identity. It may also be the responsibility of the operational manager to oversee the implementation of the ongoing marketing and promotion of the site. Thus step four is the development of a post-launch management plan.

On an annualized basis, the initial development of the site may be only a small part of the overall site budget. Administration, maintenance, and ongoing upgrades may incur noticeable additional costs that may not be part of the initial launch budget. The commitment of senior management to the Internet strategy is critical to the on time, on budget launch.

The following chapters deliver the details to launch a successful Internet strategy. The guidelines that make up the project management plan are shown in the following box.

The next two chapters will provide the framework for defining business opportunities that can drive the online objectives for a successful web site.

PROJECT MANAGEMENT GUIDELINES

To deliver a web site strategy on time and on budget, the successful Internet manager will:

1. Define focused solutions that take a proactive approach toward the delivery of concrete business objectives.
2. Develop a strategy statement with finite deliverables that are measurable and can be scaled.
3. Create a positioning strategy that reflects both internal objectives and external market conditions.
4. Build a team of professionals that leverage rather than duplicate individual skills.
5. Understand that launch is only the first step in an effective Internet strategy and that achieving business milestones is predicated on a strong ongoing management plan.

Chapter 2

Determining the Fastest Route to Internet Success

To define a business strategy that can succeed online, you should first assess current conditions. Assuming that you want to target those strategies that have the greatest market potential, you should take these five steps:

1. Define the traditional process.
2. Identify inefficiencies.
3. Address concrete solutions.
4. Define an Internet-based strategy.
5. Set clearly defined metrics.

Traditional business processes will burden even the most innovative idea. A strategy of *disintermediation*—the consumer can buy directly from the manufacturer—still requires an order-fulfillment-and-transaction process. In another scenario, targeting international markets will still require multilinguistic support. Only by documenting the traditional process can the Internet process be delivered as a definitive advantage. This chapter will deliver the process required to assess traditional business strategies against the needs of your company and to identify inefficiencies.

The Internet provides the tools to make existing business processes more efficient. Online trading is not a new business process. It is a more efficient way for the end user to complete a transaction. Many brokerage firms had the potential to dominate this space if they had identified the traditional business inefficiencies and set concrete solutions. Traditional businesses often operate in a status quo mode that enable start-ups to move into the space and steal market share. The ability to gain significant market share in today's crowded Internet space often requires either the marketing muscle of large companies or very deep investment pockets. The key to long-term market share remains in the ability to identify and to take advantage of traditional market inefficiencies.

SUCCESSFUL SITES DELIVER QUANTIFIABLE RESULTS

The launch of a successful site is predicated on a clearly defined business objective. Well-defined guidelines will include clear metrics to define success. Some successful metrics may include:

1. Increased market share through 20 percent of new customer acquisition through the web site.

2. Ten percent lower operational costs through automated 24/7 online support.

3. Fifteen percent increase in annual sales/customers through follow-on e-mail.

■ TRADITIONAL BUSINESS PROCESSES

A successful web site is one that provides tangible results consistent with predefined business objectives. The following examples outline traditional business processes that can be streamlined through an Internet solution.

BLUEPRINT

The first section of the blueprint defines the traditional business strategies and addresses the inefficiencies in these strategies.

➤ Process 1: Customer Experience

Defining the Traditional Process

It is nearly impossible for a storekeeper to gauge a customer's objectives by merely watching the customer walk into the store. Is it a casual stroll, perhaps to browse through the many offerings, or is it an educational mission to find out more about a potential purchase? Is it driven by curiosity or by purpose? And it is not an easy task for the salesclerk to quickly assess the needs and to immediately close a sale. The customer experience is based on the individual initiative. If the customer decides to make a purchase, the store/customer relationship can begin. When the clerk engages the customer in a conversation, takes credit card information, and/or notes the product purchased, the customer ceases to become an anonymous entity and a long-term customer relationship can begin. But of the many purchases made at retail level each day, how many are actually tracked in such a way as to further the next potential sale? Logistically, this has been a nearly impossible task and a significant flaw in the traditional business process.

Acting on the Inefficiency

On the Dell web site, a customer can build his or her own computer, based on genuine usage recommendations (e.g., the customer notes that he or she travels with a computer constantly, so the site may recommend a lightweight but lower-powered notebook) or on technical specifications (e.g., a multimedia specialist may request a specific videocard). In either case, the customer ends up with a system built to his or her specifications, and Dell ends up with detailed customer information that immediately forms the base for the next sale.

➤ Process 2: Sales Process

Defining the Traditional Process

The process of generating leads through direct mail campaigns has traditionally been similar to casting a very large net in the hope of catching a few small fish. First, the target audience was appropriately profiled. Then, a direct mail piece was created that would catch the attention of prospective customers. From there, companies hoped that a few of these potential customers would react—they could call the toll-free number, attend the event, forward the lead to the right person in the company who might be a better candidate. With a response rate in the low single digits, even if this process leads to a few new customers, it is highly inefficient. However, for some companies, this process has been the best possible option for new sales leads.

Acting on the Inefficiency

Kraft Foods may have begun their online strategy to feature different recipes for their products, a traditional direct mail type of approach to a site. However, the ability for end-users, specifically their most dedicated customers, to swap recipes and to exchange product-related ideas leverages the initial direct marketing approach to create a direct dialogue between customers, turning them into a highly vocal, loyal group of salespeople and enhancing the customer experience both for this loyal base and for the new customer.

➤ Process 3: Customer Support

Defining the Traditional Process

Anyone who has tried to plan an extended-family vacation is only too aware of how inefficient a process it can be. Once the destination has been selected, significant planning must still go into booking flights, selecting a hotel, finding restaurants that won't cost financial or gastro indigestion, and making sure that everyone from grandma to the baby is suitably entertained. Traditional travel agencies, although great in the planning stages, are often less effective once the trip is underway.

Acting on the Inefficiency

Etrav.com solves this customer support continuity problem through a unique combination of offline/online support. From day one, Etrav.com, with a core mission of overseas group travel, assigns a customer support representative to the trip planner, working with him or her directly to create a detailed itinerary, which is then available online for all members of the group to preview. This full-service approach to customer planning, the core objective of the online business strategy, becomes a differentiable customer experience.

➤ Process 4: Transaction Infrastructure

Defining the Traditional Process

Corporations depend on suppliers to keep their operations running smoothly. One late delivery of a part or a good can cripple the entire manufacturing process. Yet, for many companies, procuring additional goods depends, in large part, on entrenched personal relationships, a well-placed phone call at the right time, and a prenegotiated contract. A breakdown in relations can quickly shut down a corporation's operations. At the same time, sitting on excess inventory can also have a detrimental affect on a company's profit and loss as well. Streamlined processes in procurement and the transactions around them, even subtle shifts, can have a significant impact on operations.

Acting on the Inefficiency

FedEx was an early adopter to the efficiencies offered online by providing the capability for businesses (and individuals) to track shipments through a web site. As a result, the logistics process is streamlined.

➤ Process 5: Inventory Fulfillment

Defining the Traditional Process

With improvements in transportation efficiencies, the ability to send goods to farther regions has become implicitly easier. While the operating channels have opened, many corporations have not been able to satisfy regional demand

and have instead turned to a multitiered distribution system. Manufacturers may sell to distributors who, in turn, may have their own local distributors who work with purchasing agents or retailers. At each step of the process, markups are incurred, delivery time is lengthened, and efficiency is lost.

Acting on the Inefficiency

Ethan Allen, a manufacturer and private-label distributor of furniture, has been traditionally limited by its retail reach. Through the Internet, the company can promote its products in regions without a retail presence.

The next chapter will focus on how to address concrete solutions, define an Internet-based strategy, and set clearly defined metrics.

DEFINING THE BUSINESS STRATEGY

With an understanding of the flaws in the traditional business process, Internet project managers can act on market inefficiencies to deliver a differentiable strategic advantage online. To do this, the Internet manager should:

1. Assess the traditional industry inefficiencies.

2. Measure these industry inefficiencies against internal business structures.

3. Incorporate the benefits of an online strategy into solving and delivering a competitively differentiable business process.

Chapter **3**

Establishing the
Destination Point

The development of an achievable online strategy begins with the definition of clearly defined online objectives. The first step in defining these objectives is to identify the traditional process at both industry and organizational levels. The next step is to succinctly define the area of inefficiency so that an online process can be developed.

Chapter 2 presented a series of examples in which traditional industry processes were outlined. It then demonstrated how these processes were efficiently resolved through an online strategy. This chapter revisits those traditional processes and provides further details about the framework to (1) address concrete solutions, (2) define an Internet strategy, and (3) set clearly defined metrics.

■ INTERNET BUSINESS PRACTICES

Internet business practices deliver an alternative solution to the traditional, inefficient business strategy. The delivery of that solution is based on a well-defined business objective that can be realistically executed within existing business constraints. For example, a manufacturer of shoes may see the value in the delivery of customized shoes that can be sold directly to the end customer. Although the process to collect individual customer shoe preferences online may be straightforward through an online survey, inputting that information into the traditional mass-market manufacturing process may be so costly that it is an inefficient business objective.

The following five scenarios outline realistic business objectives that were successfully implemented by companies.

➤ Process 1: Customer Experience

Address Concrete Solutions

For almost any company, the ability to track customer demand will provide the immediate benefits of both deeper customer relationships and faster access to consolidated customer trends. The concrete Internet solution is to create a new mechanism to track customer demand. At the same time that the infrastructure is developed, there must be a strategy to entice the customer to share not only purchase information but also other information that will help predict future demand. Finally, clearly defined metrics must be set, perhaps by tracking the average annual amount of customer purchases through the Internet versus traditional purchase channels (such as a retail store).

Define an Internet Strategy

Fairmarket provides the back-end infrastructure to enable large corporations to incorporate auctions into their sites. Fairmarket's technology will track the bids, the sales, and the activity of the individual customer. When this is incorporated into a site like Dell, the technology provides the company with immediate entry into a new form of customer relationship—the demand and the sale of previously purchased equipment.

Set Clearly Defined Metrics

This information can be correlated with new sales activity, providing measurable metrics without adversely impacting traditional business strategies.

➤ Process 2: Sales Process

Address Concrete Solutions

The ability to turn an inquiry into a sale can be a tricky process. In the previous chapter, this process was exemplified by the low success ratio of direct-mail campaigns. Unfortunately, the success of a direct-mail campaign cannot be measured until it's completely over. If a system can be implemented by which precise metrics can be used to measure the success of a lead generation strategy in real time, offers can be modified on the fly, thereby providing more targeted and strategically more effective responses. The concrete online solution is to deliver an adjustable direct-lead-generation program through a system that targets responses with trackable results.

Define an Internet Strategy

DoubleClick, an online ad server technology, enables companies to buy advertising views based on specific demographics. The success of these advertisements, usually measured by click-throughs (the number of users who click on the ad to access the site), is provided through near real-time metrics, which enable midcampaign adjustments as necessary.

Set Clearly Defined Metrics

Incorporating this technology into a corporate lead-generation strategy provides measurable midstream results that are not available in traditional online strategies.

➤ Process 3: Customer Support

Address Concrete Solutions

Building demand around previous buying habits not only can increase customer satisfaction but also can lower production costs. In Chapter 2, the example of using the communication capabilities of the Internet to offer a more customized user experience was explored. But how can customer support impact the actual production process in a way that is both quantifiable and more efficient? Northwest Airlines (among other airlines) builds service around customer needs.

Define an Internet Strategy

A customer can request information about a specific route, for example, Boston to Seattle, online. As a form of online customer service, Northwest will send regular updates about pricing discounts and route availability between Boston and Seattle to this specific customer, building the customer relationship based on previous inquiries.

Set Clearly Defined Metrics

The results are twofold: (1) Northwest can more efficiently sell unfilled seats on specific routes, and (2) it can also gauge customer demand for specific routes by tracking customer inquiries. Over time, they can more specifically tailor their service to the needs of their customers. Results are quantifiable and offer a new level of customer support.

➤ Process 4: Transaction Infrastructure

Address Concrete Solutions

The Internet can sometimes deliver an entirely new transaction infrastructure to an industry. On-demand music delivered through the Internet is creating a significant shift in the music industry as it creates a direct consumer distribution channel as well as a new set of challenges in regard to copyright protection. Music is one of the first industries to be fundamentally impacted by distribution through the Internet because it can be compressed and distributed in a small file that can be rapidly downloaded.

Define an Internet Strategy

However, technology can also deliver the ability to track downloads, which can provide both metrics for measuring the popularity of a song and even further definition of consumer's listening habits. MP3.com provides a personalized online service in which customers' can personalize their music experience (and MP3.com can push advertisements based on music selections).

Set Clearly Defined Metrics

The new transaction infrastructure, which may be measured on number of "listens" rather than a one-time licensing fee, is fundamentally restructuring the distribution channel of the music industry. It shifts the distribution process from the purchase of a preselected music bundle on an intermediary medium to an individual music selection distributed directly to the personal system. The push of individual music and the subsequent download and access to that music provides immediate, quantifiable usage-tracking statistics.

➤ Process 5: Inventory Fulfillment

Address Concrete Solutions

The ability for a manufacturer to go directly to the consumer, cutting out the middleman, can decrease inventory and distribution costs. These cost savings may then be passed on to the end-user. For example, wineries, which are traditionally limited by U.S. law to selling only within their state through licensed sellers, can use the Internet to promote and sell to a much broader geographic base.

Define an Internet Strategy

Although the challenge remains at the regulatory level, companies like Wine.com are providing direct access to the wine produced by regional wine makers, creating a new way for these local producers to reach a broader market base.

Set Clearly Defined Metrics

Wine makers, who previously could not access a broader market, can now quantifiably distribute through a much larger distribution channel. Companies like Wine.com can help to track consumer purchase habits, to assess trends, to build customer loyalty programs, and to provide quantifiable metrics through this distribution channel.

Creating an achievable online strategy is therefore predicated on a business objective with quantifiable business results. With a clearly outlined objective, the project manager can then test his or her strategy against existing market conditions.

INTERNET OBJECTIVES

To develop an executable online strategy, the Internet manager should:

1. Review traditional processes to assess the greatest areas of opportunity.
2. Identify inefficiencies that can be addressed online.
3. Create concrete solutions that will not adversely impact the existing operational infrastructure.
4. Succinctly define the Internet-based strategy.
5. Set clearly defined metrics for success.

Part II

Assessment of Market Conditions

Chapter 4

Selecting the Passengers

The first step in assessing the market conditions is to define the users. Users are often thought of as the end consumer, but, in fact, users can include the backroom staff responsible for ensuring that the product can be delivered on time or the intermediaries who are responsible for interim steps in the process, such as shipping.

BLUEPRINT

Once the business objectives have been defined, the next section of the blueprint is to define the market conditions. Market conditions begin with the user process, which starts with the supplier and continues through to the end user. Users can generally be further subdivided into three categories: (1) suppliers, (2) employees/operations, and (3) end user. The role of each of these user groups, especially if it is different from traditional business roles, must be carefully outlined to ensure seamless execution of the online strategy. Once the roles and responsibilities of the users have been outlined, the next step is to summarize the demographic and psychographic profile of the target end user.

Petsmart.com, for example, sells pet-related products on-line. When a customer orders a product, there has to be some process with the manufacturer to pack the product and a relationship with a shipper to deliver the product. If the package should be mislabeled during packaging or the shipper should damage the product en route, then the end user will not have a satisfactory customer experience.

With a clear definition of the online business objectives, the next step is to clearly define the business process as it specifically relates to the roles and responsibilities of the various users.

■ USER PROFILE

Users will vary across an Internet plan, but they may be generally categorized into three fields: (1) the end user through the consumer distribution process, (2) the operational support team through the internal corporate functionality, and (3) the supplier through the manufacturing-and-vendor-distribution process.

➤ The End User

Because of the trumpeted reach of the Internet, it is often assumed that every business has infinite access to thousands or even millions of end users. The potential reach of the Internet is significant, but the reality is that the channel presents a highly fragmented market in which the end user is differentiated not only by his or her traditional personal preferences but also by his or her capability to navigate the medium.

A consummate consumer example is a local toy shop, a loyal customer base, and a visionary shop owner by the name of Gepeto. Gepeto knows that the market potential for an Internet toy shop is significant. Yet this toy-shop owner has built his reputation on serving a local market. Gepeto has to think first about who his end user is in an infinite marketplace. Gepeto can profile his end user from three different angles: (1) He can buy a report from a high-priced (but very reputable) research firm that will tell him exactly (or as exact as Internet statistics can be) how many toys were sold online in the past six months. (2) He can visit various toys newsgroups to find out what the marketplace is saying about toys. Both of these options will give Gepeto a general sense of whether the market is viable; but, remember, Gepeto's core market has really been his local community. (3) Gepeto may want to consider focusing his research efforts on his existing customers. Over the next six weeks, he can ask them some basic questions as they check out. *Do you own a computer? Do you go online on a regular basis? Have you bought anything online? Would you buy my toys online?* The answers may surprise him because his end user (kids) is very different from his customer (parents, friends, and relatives who have the money to buy the toys). So even if every kid in the world had access to the Internet, does that mean Gepeto has an infinite market? Not really, because even if all

---

TARGET USER RESEARCH

Both primary and secondary research will help to define the usage habits of the target end user online. Addressing whether the online strategy should be focused on penetration, acquisition, or retention will also help. Profiling the end user will also set standards, or metrics, for the development of a realistic project budget based on these strategies.

the kids in the world are online, they probably do not have enough nickels and dimes (assuming that feeding coins into the disk drive would enable an e-commerce transaction) to purchase all the toys that Gepeto would like to sell.

So, Gepeto needs to sell toys for kids whose parents (and grandparents, aunts, or uncles) are ready, willing, and able to send their credit card through the Internet. One end user, two different consumers—(1) the child who wants and (2) the adult who pays. Earlier, it was assumed that the entire universe of kids was online. Instead, assume that adults (specifically parents) are online but that the number of kids with unlimited access to the Internet is actually finite (a much likelier scenario). Gepeto has an interesting dilemma. Before, the kids would drag the adult into the little corner toyshop and stand there with that pleading look that no adult can deny until the toy was purchased. The mere visibility of his toys in a high-traffic area kept retention costs relatively low. Now, Gepeto needs to create the demand and to engage the trust of his consumer without the pleading faces of his finest salespeople. Rather than creating an infinite opportunity for Gepeto, the Internet has created a fragmented consumer market. Even though the end user remains the same, kids, the relationship between the seller and the buyer has fundamentally changed. The long-term retention costs may be low, but Gepeto needs to develop a strategy to reach a finite audience that will justify the costs of developing the online strategy.

DEFINITION OF THE END USER

Careful definition of the end user up front can help deliver more effective results in the long term.

Because of the rapid acceptance rate of the Internet, Gepeto's consumers may vary dramatically in their access, use, and comfort level with the Internet, creating another level of complexity in his relationship with his end users. Defining this technical proficiency as a "byte profile," his end users' access may be determined by how they log on to the Internet—whether though a home modem connection, cable access, or a T1 connection at the office. The consumer may be a technical innovator, downloading the latest browser version and plug-in applications, or a late adopter, using a functionally obsolete browser to view the web. She or he may be a "web runner," online all day with long-term commerce relationships, on a first-name basis with the FedEx delivery person, and with a First Virtual credit card. Or the consumer may be slowly emptying the attic through an online auction. Whatever the profile, Gepeto needs to recognize the factors in these attributes that may set wildly divergent expectations for his online store.

Not all scenarios complicate the sales process like that of Gepeto. A flip-side opportunity is the restocking of office products in large corporations. The traditional process of office supply replenishment may require the office worker to send a requisition form to an office manager, who accumulates these orders until a critical mass is reached and a discounted bulk order is placed. If instead of funneling the order through a central resource, individual workers are empowered to purchase directly (based on a preexisting corporate account with an office supply house), then the process of consolidation, order entry, and distribution is compressed. Herein lies an example of where a shift in consumer purchasing power (albeit with the same end user) enables increased efficiencies via the office supply house and its corporate consumer.

Staples.com has begun to set up external requisition systems that address this issue in both small and large corporations.

The disassociation of the end user and the customer through the Internet may require a fundamental shift in the customer relationship. Recognition of and preparation for this shift create the framework for an online strategy that is responsive to rather than inconsistent with the needs of the end user.

Once both the demographic and the technical profile of the end user is defined, the next step is to assess the role of the internal employee within the new Internet process.

➤ The Operational Support Team

With the introduction of a new business process through the Internet, traditional internal roles may change. Customer support through a phone center may be supplemented or replaced by e-mail or online dialogues such as the LivePerson system that was discussed in an earlier chapter. This shift may impact the traditional role of the customer support sales center, which may need additional training to appropriately respond to customer requests through e-mail. Alternatively, an integrated, online, knowledge-management system may replace some of the traditional customer support requirements, creating layoffs. In either case, if the end-to-end user process is defined up front, these types of shifts or training requirements are anticipated and incorporated up front into the project blueprint.

The following true case exemplifies what can happen when a smart Internet strategy fails due to lack of definition of internal roles and responsibilities: A large corporation developed an online strategy to generate awareness and ultimately to deliver qualified leads for a new service rollout. Support at the corporate level drove the project launch. Information Technology (IT) was brought in to support the plan. The product manager was also committed to the strategy. Rollout was seamless, and the site was launched. Marketing begins and, in short order, the leads started rolling in. Everything was flawlessly executed. Weeks go by and the leads continued to develop. But nothing has happened. None of the leads was generating customers. The process was backtracked throughout the system. The culprit? New business development was the responsibility of an employee who was never educated or empowered to act on the new process. In fact, that person was not even connected to the e-mail group. Instead, each new lead was printed in hard copy and sent to him. The strategy failed because there was no education or realignment of internal job responsibilities as a part of the overall strategy.

If the Internet creates new or different responsibilities for individual employees, how is this reconciled with or accounted for in the overall business plan? The success of a plan is as dependent on the smooth implementation of internal business processes as it is on the selection of the technical infrastructure. Does the online process replace or supplement existing processes? If it replaces an existing process, then there may be substantial interim costs involved in the retraining of the staff.

Another example of internal user processes is within a software company that makes the proactive decision to offer product upgrades through the Internet. While the immediate efficiency of the online downloads may be apparent, there is still a level of internal training and process reallocation that needs to take place. The download process itself may require a different type of technical support as subtle differences in computer systems may create snags in the process. So, while the downloading process may speed software upgrades to the end user, it may create the additional cost of technical support.

Shifts in the roles and the responsibilities of the internal team as a result of the Internet strategy will also impact the efficiency of the online process. By addressing the role of the employees within the Internet process up front, the project is more likely to meet the overall business objectives. To launch on time and on budget and to effectively meet the overall business objectives, it is important to include a definition of the roles and the responsibilities of the employees as part of the user process within the project blueprint. This may also include training and administrative strategies to ensure the ongoing execution of the online program.

Once the target profile of the end user has been defined, and the roles and responsibilities of the internal team in the online process have been assessed, the third primary user base to assess is the supplier.

➤ The Supplier

For years, if a consumer wanted to purchase a car, he or she would go to the local car dealership and negotiate for a car. The consumer, regardless of whether he or she was buying a Hyundai or a Ferrari, would establish a relationship with the dealer who would work directly with the manufacturer.

What happens when the consumer can go directly to the manufacturer and bypass the dealer? Does this dissolve the relationship between the vendor and the manufacturer? Does it modify the leverage between the vendor and the manufacturer? Or does it redefine the vendor and the manufacturer as competitors?

If the online strategy is to deliver to market more efficiently, then, by enabling the customer to order direct through a web site, cutting out the dealer may seem the logical solution to the strategy. Some manufacturers had plans to buy dealerships as a way to shift control in the end-user relationship. However, GM's 1999 plan to buy 700 dealerships or about 10 percent of the company's total dealer network, was met by significant resistance by traditional dealers, and the plans were ultimately dropped.

But does shifting the distribution process always create the most effective end solution when developing an online strategy? Many of the major automobile manufacturers are restructuring their online strategies to bypass the middleman and allow the end user to select and purchase a car directly from their site. Without the dealer, who is responsible for servicing the car? Does the manufacturer create a new service channel to maintain the car? Who encourages the consumer to upgrade to a new car in year three instead of in year four? What is the implicit value that the customer places on knowing the service team? Or does the ownership of a car simply become a highly commoditized purchase?

Rather than a disintermediation strategy, the Internet creates a new opportunity to maximize the long-term relationship with the customer by empowering the dealer to create a stronger, customized relationship. If information about a car becomes widely available through the Internet, then chances are that that same information about other cars becomes widely available. A logical conclusion is that the purchase of a car becomes a commoditized experience of price and features. And this could be the case, if a car never required an oil change or a brake check. It is also the case if the consumer doesn't go through a lifestyle change, such as a new child or a new job that changes the daily commuting schedule. A commoditized relationship does not factor in these details that can define the next sale (and point of profit) for the vendor.

Cutting out the dealer negates the customized relationship. By not conveying appropriate value on this relationship,

---

ROLE OF THE SUPPLIER

The third user in the Internet process is the supplier, or vendor. The traditional versus the online relationship of the supplier/vendor should be carefully addressed as part of the user process. Perceived short-term benefits of cutting out the middleman may be offset by long-term costs of customer service and retention strategies. Careful definition of the needs of the three major users—end user, employee/internal team, and vendor/supplier—in the online process is thus critical to the success of meeting the online business objectives.

---

the benefits of the immediate sale may be lost due to the diminished loyalty for the second sale. A regional dealer in New England recognizes this shift in access to information and has taken a proactive rather than reactive approach to its relationship with its customers. The home page of the dealer's web site emphasizes service (in addition to sales), such as the promotion of a free oil change when scheduling a service appointment online. Another example is the option to join the dealer's e-mail list (with a privacy policy clearly stated). The benefits of the e-mail list are clearly defined as receiving notices of sales, services, and parts specials. The dealer's proactive approach to online customer support creates a more satisfied, long-term customer, which ultimately benefits the manufacturer.

Thus, the vendor/supplier roles in the Internet process are also critical to implementing a successful online strategy. By addressing the potential supply chain opportunities and leveraging these opportunities across the distribution channel, more effective results may be achieved.

■ NEEDS ANALYSIS

Once the multiple users are defined, the next step is to prioritize their impact within the overall strategic statement and to communicate a detailed needs analysis that can be integrated into the timely development and delivery of the online process.

➤ Integration

The simplest and least effective response to integrating the needs of the various users is to rank one group as more important than the others and ignore the needs of the rest.

A more effective strategy is to create a process chart in which each of the roles of the users are clearly outlined. In the case of the local retailer, the process in its simplest form may look something like Figure 4.1.

While this process may be streamlined through the Internet, it has not been totally automated and still requires human interaction to ensure its completion. If at any step of

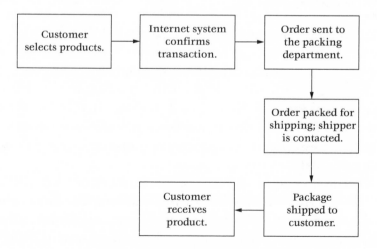

Figure 4.1 Sample process chart.

the process there is not adequate user support (regardless of whether that user is the customer, the employee, or the vendor), the efficiencies anticipated by the carefully outlined process may fail because of inadequate support processes.

For example, if orders exceed the ability to ship or simply cannot be filled from inventory, as happened during the 1999 holiday season, then the process cannot be completed despite the most sophisticated Internet solutions.

BLUEPRINT

A user process chart outlines the various roles and responsibilities in a flowchart. When incorporated into the second section of the project blueprint, this chart will provide a succinct road map to ensure that the launch strategies are successfully met.

➤ Alienation

Responding to the needs of one user base while ignoring the impact on other extends beyond the challenge of a local toy shop. A large manufacturer of construction vehicles recognizes the inherent value of the direct-to-customer reach of the Internet. Prior to the Internet, influencing the end consumer was more efficiently achieved through a middleman who could sustain the heavy costs of maintaining a direct customer relationship.

Via the Internet and a database-driven customer-profiling system, the traditional costs of maintaining the direct customer relationship diminishes. Business logic would then conclude that the opportunity of a direct-to-customer service channel via the Internet would benefit both the manufacturer and the customer.

Although cost efficiencies may be gained with this direct-to-customer approach, what is the impact on service when the traditional middleman is removed from the equation? Service demands shift from the middleman to the manufacturer. Because the customer can no longer call the friendly-down-the-street distributor, a call (or e-mail) will be placed directly to the manufacturer. To offer the same level of service as a local distributor, a representative from the manufacturer may need to do an on-site inspection to assess the appropriate solution to the problem. Having alienated the traditional service base, the manufacturer must build an Internet service-support channel or risk losing a loyal customer to a service-friendly distributor. Alienation of the distributor places a new burden of demand on the manufacturer. And, who is the logical service support provider but the very middleman who was removed from the channel in the first place. By not fully recognizing the needs and, in this case, pivotal roles of the various constituents, the online strategy may end up replacing one set of inefficiencies with another.

➤ Incorporate the Role of Each User into the Site Blueprint

To create an online strategy that both meets the overall business objectives and also is functional, the ongoing roles of each user in the project plan must be addressed.

BLUEPRINT

Section two of the project blueprint should detail the process flow, including the ongoing roles and responsibilities of the users, regardless of whether that user is the end customer, the employee, the middleman, or the supplier.

■ GOALS

At this stage, the broad business objectives outlined in the first part of the blueprint should be further defined to become concrete process goals. For example, if the business objective is to offer live online support (e.g., LivePerson), the processes to train live support personnel should be added to the overall blueprint. By combining the overall goals with specific process deliverables, the Internet architecture begins to solidify.

In a true case example, a large manufacturer decides to market directly to the consumer to sell a specific part. However, that part will then be installed by the local distributor. This objective is then broken down into a series of smaller process goals that reflect user requirements.

> ➤ *Process Goal 1*—The manufacturer creates a web site that features the product benefits process but also provides local distributor information depending on user Zip code. The manufacturer and the distributor negotiate an arrangement (such as shared installation fees) for each installation based on leads generated through the manufacturer's site.

> ➤ *Process Goal 2*—Leaders are tracked by the distributor representative through a predetermined code. The customer receives the same level of service regardless of point of purchase (traditional or manufacturer web site).

> ➤ *Process Goal 3*—The manufacturer and the distributor establish an Internet-based reconciliation process to track and to credit web site generated sales on a monthly basis.

By dividing the overall business objective into smaller user process goals, the individual roles and responsibilities of the Internet strategy are predefined.

■ SCHEDULE

Defining the process goals for the users up front will create a longer-term, sustainable (and successful) online strategy. However, it is important to balance the complete solution with shorter steps because the Internet moves very quickly. Implementing the LivePerson technology into a customer support process is a great example of a process goal. However, six or nine months from now, mass market use of voice over the Internet may create an entirely new platform for customer support. Process goals tie into the launch schedule as an iterative process, achieving the business milestones as outlined in the longer-term objectives. As these milestones are met, the goals change, and the roles and responsibilities of the users evolve as well.

EVALUATE AND ITERATE

The user process chart should be continually evaluated as business objectives are met and market conditions change. In this way, the process flow will be naturally evolving as part of the Internet process rather than hindering or slowing down market opportunities. A 90-day time frame for review becomes an iterative schedule for assessment and modifications.

When Yahoo! began, one of its differentiating services was the reviewing of sites by human editors. These users were trained to assess listings as they were submitted to the directory. As the popularity of Yahoo! grew and the number of listings increased, editors were required to review more sites; thus the demands within the original process evolved over time. Subsequently, Yahoo! partnered with an automated site directory to supplement the personal listing services, managing their growth and maintaining their market position over time.

By setting the process goals in a 90-day time frame, the overall business objectives are continually being evaluated, and users are able to support evolving needs. The process then becomes one of multiple iterations based on smaller goals rather than internal development with one final goal. Making the users part of the process (as outlined in the earlier example) may accelerate the market realization absorption rate.

■ CREATE AN ONLINE STRATEGY FOR A GROWING BASE

In a traditional business strategy, select focus groups may be brought in at various stages to test the business concept. Online, these test focus groups become microcosms of sustainable market strategies.

A targeted online strategy may begin with a select group of users, whether they are end users, vendors, intermediaries, or any other constituent base. The next step then is to create an online environment in which they can communicate with one another (e.g., chat rooms, user groups, web conferences). If the demand is to gain access to more information, give them access to that information online and measure their response. As the interaction increases, enlarge the focus group to include more users. For example, if the original user base (perhaps a group of distributors) demands more efficient access to product specifications, create an environment for the product engineers to post information and get feedback. The dialogue of the original focus group now expands from management to manufacturer to distributor to engineer. Bring in other parties as the community demands. Invite a few key customers and track the results. As the community grows, it evolves from a traditional focus group to a market microcosm. With rapid evolution, this market microcosm becomes a market maker and the opportunity presents itself.

■ THE OPPORTUNITY

The next challenge is scale. Basing success on set subgroups of users may or may not scale to a financially feasible market opportunity.

Hence, it is critical to manage and to measure the flow of demand. What may have begun as a strategy to sell direct to market may evolve into a focus on up selling traditional customers by developing a scalable, customer profile database.

DEFINE THE USERS

Once the overall business objectives are defined, the project manager can begin to solidify the details that will actively ensure a seamless online process. The first strategy is to define the various users and their roles in the online process. Users include customers, employees, and vendors/suppliers. When defining the roles and responsibilities of the users, the project manager should consider the following:

1. Create a finite profile of each user and the role each group will play in the online process.

(Continued)

(Continued)

2. Succinctly define each role within a process flow-chart that will be incorporated into the site blueprint; recognize that the role will evolve over time.

3. Create a strategy for growth in which the role of the user may evolve over time based on changing demand and on the achievement of previously defined business objectives.

Chapter 5

Leapfrogging Competitive Barriers

After translating the internal business objectives into specific user needs, the next step is thoroughly assessing the market alternatives for the target user(s). By thoroughly analyzing the competitive landscape, the business risk of the site launch is decreased.

Every path to an Internet launch should begin with the assumption that someone else in the business world has already, at least in part, begun to lay the groundwork for a similar online strategy. If it is assumed that the idea is so original that there is no existing business or project model, then the project plan immediately loses a valuable edge that such a learning curve would provide, and launching the site quickly and effectively poses a greater challenge. A critical step, then, is checking out your competition. Look to see who's out there, from the stodgy corporation weighed down by a legacy system to the kid next door who happens to get financed by a very indulgent rich uncle.

The next deliverable in the project blueprint is a competitive positioning strategy that details the relative strengths and weaknesses of the key market players. The following competitive market guidelines will lay the groundwork to:

➤ Define the key variables that will assess the strengths and weaknesses of the competition.

➤ Pinpoint the competition.

➤ Create a competitive positioning strategy.

COMPETITIVE ANALYSIS

A thorough understanding of both current market conditions and strategies of key market players is critical for the successful launch of an online strategy. An assessment of these market conditions will include:

1. An analysis of the top industry sites.

2. A summary of offline market conditions to help predict upcoming online strategies.

3. An offensive competitive positioning strategy.

The most competitive online positioning strategy for an individual company may be to deliver an industrywide solution. In the case of sites like esteel.com and PlasticsNet.com, industry veterans used their individual skills and expertise to create a consolidated online market. In 1995, two brothers, Tim and Nick Stojka, did a broad competitive assessment of their family's business in the plastics industry. Instead of launching a site to solely target their traditional end user, they made the foresighted decision to create an online marketplace to buy and sell goods in the $370 billion plastics industry. Their competitive assessment of a market opportunity based on the supplier as the end user has enabled them to become one of the online market leaders in the plastics industry.

■ DEFINE THE KEY VARIABLES

When they analyzed their industry online, the Stojka brothers discovered that the most significant variable that drove the success of any one player in their industry was its individual leverage within the highly fragmented industry distribution channel. To see this opportunity and to weigh that variable as the greatest opportunity, they had to have a thorough understanding of existing market conditions.

Using that successful positioning strategy as a benchmark to analyze market variables, the following hypothetical case illustrates the process to prioritize the key competitive variables in an online strategy. A certain travel agency, a traditional leader in its local market, has long dominated the number-two position, based on gross revenue generated per customer. Because leisure travel is usually an annual event, initial customers acquisition costs are offset by ongoing customer loyalty that can generate an annuity for years to come. To minimize the high cost of customer acquisition, the agency's traditional growth has come through the acquisition of smaller agencies in adjacent geographic regions where there is the greatest likelihood of name-brand recognition. Constraints in corporate growth were based primarily on the ability to service more customers in a way that would meet or exceed that provided by the acquired company. The opportunity to inexpensively promote the brand name in any given region was the first step in acquiring the competition.

At the same time, service, the travel agency's key differentiator from other travel services, was based on (1) the ability to deliver personal travel preferences based on previous buying patterns (most customers were assigned to one customer representative) and (2) the ability to find the best prices and to respond quickly to customer needs. The travel agency was not able to compete on convenience, however, as the customer representatives at the travel agency worked a traditional 9 to 6 workweek schedule. While skewing heavily to the service side, the agency would traditionally lose competitively against any service that offered 24-hour-a-day, 7-day-a-week (24/7), convenience, including customer direct calls to airlines and/or hotel reservation systems.

The agency is now considering expanding its market reach through the Internet, but it must first assess the needs of its customers to determine its competitive positioning strategy. Their key competitive variables are customer acquisition and personalized service.

To date, the agency's new customer acquisition has been based on a regional growth strategy. The Internet theoretically negates the regional constraints of servicing the customer, but it places additional stress on the ability to offer a high level of personal service. Within personal service, there are two existing user needs plus one potential service solution that can be efficiently delivered only through the Internet. The first need that the company addresses is the ability to provide highly personalized customer service. With a commitment to long-term satisfaction, the agency delivers a deep customer relationship. Translating this into an online environment, the agency may commit significant resources to an online customer profiling system in which both the customer and the representative can build a detailed database of customer preferences that will lead to smarter, more efficient decisions in the future. In other words, the *first need* is migrating customized service on the web through personalized profiles.

The *second need* that the agency addresses is the ability to get the best deal. Online, this may be delivered by creating a mechanism by which the customer can send a request weighting the value of a series of parameters (price, timing, convenience) and allowing the online system to provide the best solution.

Finally, the *third need* is the ability to deliver 24/7 responses that retain the high level of customer service.

COMPETITIVE POSITIONING

It is critical to develop the corporate online strategy in the context of the online marketplace. As a new distribution channel, the opportunities to offer a differentiated service may be different from traditional online opportunities. Compare the overall benefits and shortcomings of the channel to the traditional corporate position.

By defining the historic relationship with the customer and focusing on the needs that can better be addressed through an online exchange, the travel agency can begin to develop a competitive positioning strategy based on targeted results. In a general business use, needs define the competitive marketplace and not the general opportunity. By focusing on these needs, the travel agency can deliver by leveraging intrinsic strengths rather than by merely responding to a perceived market opportunity.

■ PINPOINT THE COMPETITION

After defining the variables that will have the most significant impact on the competitive position, the next step is determining the opportunity that will enable the company to be the most aggressive competitor in the online market-place.

The competition can be defined on two planes, (1) horizontal and (2) vertical. For the regional travel agency, *horizontal competition* comes from the traditional competitor—other travel agencies, outlets, even direct-to-suppliers such as airlines. *Vertical competition,* as discussed in more detail later in this chapter, is presented by those services that provide information that can impact the target user's decision-making process.

HORIZONTAL VERSUS VERTICAL COMPETITION

Because of direct access to the end user, competition online may be both horizontal and vertical. Horizontal competition is the traditional competition of similar companies offering similar services. Vertical competition is the nontraditional competition that may occur throughout the supply chain as direct access to the end user becomes less expensive to achieve online.

Online, the traditional competition—wholesalers and direct customer outlets—are a mere click away from the travel agency site. Thus, the ability to provide the best deal as efficiently as possible becomes an even more critical offering through the web site. The agency may want to consider, in fact, if it is still appropriate or even cost effective to compete online in this area. Instead, the agency may place lower priority on the variable of delivering the best deal by emphasizing customized, one-on-one service.

The ability to deliver detailed customer profiling, specifically based on historic buying patterns, can prove a distinct advantage in the overall competitive positioning strategy. Leveraging the historical customer travel information housed in the existing customer database creates a defensible competitive strategy online because no other horizontal competitor has access to that information. However, this data may not yet be available in a form that is conducive to the end customer who, through the web site, may not only want to view his or her personal information but may also want to access it through a different process than traditionally available. One simple example would be that the historic record shows a customer preference for an aisle seat on planes. Length of a specific upcoming flight may create a desire for a window seat instead. The online customer profile should be flexible enough to account for these changes at both the administrative and the customer level. Any competitive web site that provides this flexibility, with or without the advantage of historic profiling information, will be competitively positioned against the existing system. Here, there is renewed emphasis on the personal customer relationship with an understanding of the potential costs to retrofit the legacy systems to respond directly to customer needs.

Round-the-clock service, a low priority in the traditional business model, may become a primary competitive variable in the online marketplace as automated access to information becomes a more realistic deliverable online. For the travel agency, there may now be two levels of customer service: (1) Customers may contact representatives in real time, that is, for instantaneous feedback; (2) Customers may send a question to support through the web site, which will be answered via e-mail in 24 hours or through a customer callback.

Online, the end user also has more access to alternative resources, the vertical competition, that may not be as readily apparent in the traditional market. For example, a traveler who wishes to book a trip to the Amazon River region may not go to his or her travel agent first online. Instead, he or she may first visit Amazon-related sites. Having previewed two or three, the traveler may independently compile a list of places to explore, a role traditionally affiliated with the travel agent who can provide "expert" advice. The information-rich sites thus become a new competitive threat to the traditional travel agent, as a source of information creating the vertical competition noted earlier.

PARTNERING OPPORTUNITIES

Because competition in the online market is both horizontal and vertical, an attractive online strategy may require partnering with nontraditional affiliates.

Because of easy online access, the traveler may then continue to research logistics through traditional competitors (easily accessible online) such as a site that provides information about airfare, either an airline or maybe a site that guarantees low airfares. From there, the traveler may visit the site of a hotel chain or try to find accommodations from a regional site. In any case, by unbundling the experience, the traveler visits perhaps a half-dozen sites that compete both horizontally and vertically with the travel agency.

Does this mean that the travel agency simply can't compete against all of the potential competitors online? Rather than responding defensively and narrowly outlining the service options, the travel agency should identify the greatest strengths of the traditional customer experiences and leverage them within the site. If most customers are travel customers, then partnership or affiliation with business travel services, such as airline frequent flyer programs or car rental sites, make the online experience of visiting the agency site far more effective than visiting and booking services (and repetitively reentering transaction data) at each site. The travel agency can leverage the access to information on the web and combine it with the historical customer information to offer an even more customized service to customers.

The travel agency, in positioning against its vertical competitors online, can offer similar services or can partner with select sites to create a common resource, often known as a "vortal" (vertical portal). For example, if many of the travel agency's traditional customers travel to South America, the travel agency site may include a linked list to reputable sites that provide information specifically about South America. In this way, the travel agency retains its position as a booking resource but also forms partnerships and alliances to empower their customers to easily access additional information of personal interest.

■ CREATE A COMPETITIVE POSITIONING STRATEGY

After prioritizing the competitive variables and outlining the potential areas of both horizontal and vertical competition,

RESEARCH

The final step in completing the online competitive positioning strategy is to complete a due diligence analysis through primary and secondary research methodologies. Research should also include a detailed assessment of competitive sites based upon design, content and functionality.

the next step is completing the due diligence that will finalize the competitive positioning strategy. This due diligence includes research at both the primary and the secondary level.

➤ Primary Research

Ask the customers what they want. Very often, the easiest customer to satisfy through the Internet will be the customer with whom there is an established relationship of trust and service. Does this mean that the online service will ultimately cannibalize the traditional means of doing business? The answer to that question depends on the overall business strategy. Satisfied customers who have an established rapport with the company will most likely have the greatest insight into how the company can better service their needs. Also, customers who have been asked for feedback from the beginning will have a vested interest in the company's success in the future.

Primary research can be as simple as a quick follow-up question at the end of an average customer phone call: Do you have e-mail (validating the online usage of the customer)? Do you currently purchase products online, or do you plan to in the future (validating the comfort level with online transactions)? Would you be interested in filling out an online service that includes a raffle for two airline tickets (not only validating comfort level with providing personal information but also establishing online customer service)? These questions are all quick and relatively easy ways to find out about online competitive opportunities.

A less distracting (but a summarily less-response-oriented) program may be a direct-mail program. Ideally, this may be analyzed against a direct e-mail program to compare response and feedback.

However, the most effective primary research may be to select a cross section of customers (active, new, prospects) and engage them as part of the development team. For example, a select group of preferred customers may become part of the test group that will access, review, and provide feedback about the web site as various stages of development are completed. Key customers who are made a part of the process early on establish deep customer roots that may have a positive impact on differentiating the service as it evolves. This feedback can then become a primary resource in determining how to best position the site online.

➤ Secondary Research

Secondary research includes offline and online research, as well as a detailed assessment of historic partners who may prove to be competitors online.

Offline Research

Offline research may begin by reviewing trade magazines and association news, attending industry conferences, and exploring any relevant government reports. This research should be focused in two primary areas: (1) reviewing the strategies of the traditional market players to understand their strengths and weaknesses in the online marketplace and (2) assessing nontraditional competitors who may compete for the same target customers in the online marketplace. For example, the local edition of the regional newspaper would not traditionally be considered a competitor of the travel agency. Although the newspaper may provide editorial content rich in travel opportunities, it does not have the technical capability (nor the business focus) to actually reserve the trip at the end of the article. But, with an online edition and a mix of the appropriate technology, the newspaper can rather seamlessly either host or partner to offer travel services. In the competitive battlefield for target customers, the number of potential competitors may increase substantially.

However, the entrenched relationships with the traditional service providers will still carry weight in the online marketplace. Reviewing publicly available information, such as annual reports or analyst recommendations, may provide some insight into competitive strategies. Significant investments in technology may also be indicative of an upcoming launch.

Online Research

Online research will include an assessment of potential competitors. One suggested strategy is to enter select keywords into the top online search engines. Results of these searches (each of which begin with the top 10 to 20 responses in each category) will provide immediate insight into who has some of the most visible positions in this specific market niche. Note also the banner advertising results at the top of the page to determine who may be purchasing these keywords.

Create a running list of these results (to be used in the future as a starting point for future competitive analysis), and track the following:

Company
Web address
Physical address
Phone number
Contact name
E-mail contact

Then, assess each site based on content, design, and functionality:

➤ *Content.* What type of information does the web site provide? Is it current? Can it be customized? Is there a "member-" or "subscriber-only" section, which may be indicative of customized service? What are the general sections of the site? How deep/broad are the sections?

➤ *Design.* Is the site aesthetically pleasing? As compared to other sites, an informal ranking system may be helpful. Is it busy with many embedded applets, or is it straightforward and simple in its design? Is the navigation easy to use? Are there any dead ends in the site? Is the site rich in text, or is it heavy in graphics? (A helpful exercise may be to list a group of key competitive sites and then review them for design consistency.) Do certain colors dominate the sites? Are photos used as a primary feature of the sites, or do they take secondary emphasis to text?

The end objective of the exercise is to develop guidelines for what creates an appealing site within the specific market niche. These guidelines can then lay the groundwork for the graphic design of the target site. For example, a comparison of the Pepsi Cola site with the Coca-Cola site in early 2000 showed that the design of each site indicates a distinct market focus. The Pepsi site targets an entertaining experience with direct navigation to a series of "challenges," while company information is given secondary priority on the site. The main links from the Coca-Cola home page, however, are about the company, investor relations, and news at Coke.

➤ *Functionality.* How customized is the experience? Is there online registration? If a visitor does register online, what does he or she receive in exchange for giving certain information (yes, it is critical to "act as the customer" at each site, registering for information, signing up for services)? What about transactions— does the site accept credit card transactions? What is the confirmation process? What is the return policy? What about future sales? Can a visitor go online, review prior purchasing history, and confirm or modify past transactions to facilitate future sales? What is the process for recommending follow-on services (e.g., returning to the travel example, when a flight is reserved, the site automatically suggests reserving a car)? How easy is it to change and/or add customer profile information (e.g., traveling with a small child and accommodating specific needs)?

As each of the criteria is compared against existing sites, then what may have started as a seemingly endless list of competitors will probably whittle down to maybe one or two dozen.

Recognition of the competition thus leads to the development of a full-scale positioning strategy.

■ CREATING A COMPETITIVE POSITIONING CHART

Based on the traditional industry position as well as on a general assessment of the online marketplace, a competitive positioning chart can summarize the most opportunistic competitive position for the company.

In the case of the travel agency as noted earlier, it is competing on two primary variables: (1) customer services and (2) price. Generally, the two are correlated such that low price limits the ability to provide high-end customized service.

Online, the business focus may shift from price to the ability to offer a higher level of customer service via technology.

ONLINE COMPETITION

The final step in creating an offensive competitive positioning strategy is charting the key competition, both horizontal and vertical, based on the primary competitive variables. By charting the relative position of each competitor, based on the key variables, market clusters and areas of opportunity can be clearly defined.

Competitors with existing technology can offer a lower price but may not be able to leverage long-term experience for a stronger customer relationship. Thus, the competitive positioning of the travel agency, when plotting technology against service, may look something like Figure 5.1.

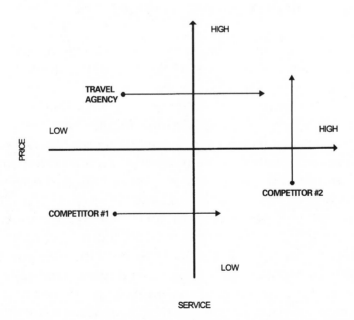

Figure 5.1 Core competitive positioning strategy—travel agency.

The ideal position from a competitive standpoint is to offer a high level of customer service based on long-term customer relationships and to offer it through technology that builds on historic customer preferences. The key differentiation for the travel agency is to leverage these historic preferences. Alternatively, a technology-rich site may have the infrastructure to deliver customized information but needs to build the customer relationships to offer a unique experience based on previous purchases. Finally, the alternative information sites may offer some level of customer service but little in the way of technology without an integration partner. Similarly, the traditional competitors, other travel agencies, may be positioned on the competitive chart based on their core strengths.

■ PLANNING FOR THE FUTURE

Existing competition can at least be catalogued and compressed when looking back at the traditional marketplace. But what about those future players, the ideas hatched out of garages and basements that shoot into a dominant market position? When you look at some of the most successful .com start-ups, a pattern does begin to emerge. Most often, it is some inefficiency in the market that allows these young companies to become what has been qualified as overnight successes. Priceline gained rapid market space in the online travel industry because it competed on customer-driven pricing strategies. Mapquest, while not a direct player in the traditional travel market, does provide critical destination services in the form of directions and maps. Online bookstores, like Amazon.com, do offer one-stop service for travel information. What all of these sites have in common is that they looked at the traditional factors that influenced the travel experience and offered a different level of efficiency through the Internet.

So how can a traditional player anticipate and position against future opportunities like this? By staying close to the needs of the customer and listening (and acting on) their feedback, the traditional player builds an online infrastructure not driven solely by supply-side opportunities but based on customer-driven demands. The Internet thus becomes a forum for exchange and opportunity in which feedback and response become an iterative process.

Because of the liquid state of the Internet, competitive strategy can no longer be an annual housekeeping event. Instead, it is a daily part of the ongoing strategy to maintain a strong position on the Internet. Maintaining and nurturing customer relationships is a key part of this strategy, as is becoming a regular customer of competitive sites.

COMPETITIVE POSITIONING

Once the user process has been succinctly defined, the next step is to complete a thorough assessment of the online market through a competitive positioning strategy. The steps to complete a thorough competitive positioning strategy include:

1. Defining the key competitive variables.

2. Assessing both the traditional horizontal competition and the potential vertical competition.

3. Completing both primary and secondary research, which includes a detailed assessment of competitive sites based on design, content, and functionality.

(Continued)

(Continued)

4. Creating a positioning chart as a guideline to the overall market opportunity.

5. Committing to an ongoing strategy of assessment and review to maintain the most effective competitive position.

Chapter 6

Creating a Smooth Customer Ride

Beginning with the overall business objectives, an effective online strategy requires a detailed understanding of the target user needs. These needs are then compared to the current market conditions to create a viable market opportunity. However, even the most technically viable market opportunity does not guarantee a successful online strategy unless it can deliver a long-term, sustainable change in target user habits. One of the most significant challenges in delivering an online strategy is creating an environment in which the target user can immediately recognize the value of the online offering.

For example, consider the millions of e-mails that are now sent every day as an accepted form of communication. Yet the widespread use of e-mail has only occurred in recent years. What was the awareness strategy that created the mass market demand for e-mail? How did those users come to accept e-mail as a viable and valuable alternative for corresponding in both business and personal settings? What were the initial conditions that created the incentive to use e-mail for the first time? How did the short-term change evolve into a long-term habit?

Developing a sustainable online strategy means creating the awareness, delivering a quantifiable service, and changing the traditional habits of the target user. This chapter will provide a framework for creating user experiences that successfully change user habits, the final step in defining the market conditions that will enable the successful launch of a site.

CUSTOMER VALUE

The final step in assessing the market conditions that will deliver a successful launch is creating a value proposition that will entice the target user, complete a high-level awareness campaign, and develop a long-term retention strategy. By defining these conditions as part of the project blueprint, the project evolves from a one-time event—the launch—to a long-term business strategy.

In the case of e-mail, access to the Internet and ease of use in sending e-mail, driven in part through the protocols introduced in the early 1990s, enabled more users to rapidly send e-mail. This, in turn, drove more users to consider e-mail as a viable means of communication. Companies like America Online (AOL) built awareness based on ease of use and low-cost access. As an inexpensive option to telephone conversations and a more efficient communication than mail or fax, the initial acquisition created immediate long-term users because the inherent value was immediately obvious to the target user. Companies that provided the infrastructure, created the communication pathways, or enabled low-cost and easy e-mail access capitalized on the widespread adaptation of e-mail communication. Creating the immediate value proposition—ease of use, low-cost access—enabled the online strategy to succeed. But how do you create that similar value proposition when the benefits may not be as immediately obvious or when the migration path may take longer or be more complicated? Delivering a focused positioning strategy requires the following steps:

➤ Understanding customer expectations

➤ Managing customer relationships

➤ Developing customer profiles

➤ Creating customer awareness

➤ Sustaining the customer relationship

➤ Building long-term customer strategies

■ UNDERSTANDING CUSTOMER EXPECTATIONS

One of the most effective online strategies is leveraging existing relationships by offering enhanced services. For a supplier, this may mean sharing inventory-tracking online with a customer to ensure a faster turnaround of replenished stock. Historically, restocking may have occurred only when an observant purchasing agent noticed that the supply of a stock was low and called the supplier, who would rush to refill the order. Online, a system can be set up in which both the purchasing agent and the supplier can track product inventory. In turn, the supplier can more efficiently meet the consumer's supply and demand needs.

Consider the example of a company sending a package to someone. Sending a package requires postage. Before postage meters, companies would either have to go to the post office or have a supply of stamps (and a scale) on hand. With the introduction of postage meters, companies could prebuy an amount of "postage" (their "supply") from which they could then print stamps to place on their packages. Companies would have to buy (or lease) the meter and a scale and establish an account with the postal service. Once the credit in the account were gone, the company would have to restock their virtual inventory of stamps. Today, companies like Stamps.com work directly with the United States Postal Service to deliver the ability to set up an online account and print stamps directly through a standard office printer. Stamp purchases are debited either directly from a credit card or through automatic withdrawal from a bank account, offering a clear value add to the target user.

In addition to offering a clear benefit to the target user, Stamps.com also delivers a direct benefit to the supplier. Stamps.com has created the process to streamline the purchase and use of the services provided by the U. S. Postal Service, enabling it to compete more effectively with package delivery services like FedEx.

The five-step process outlined earlier, to enable a longer-term, more sustainable relationship based on the shift in user habits, begins with understanding customer expectations.

Banking is a strong example of shifts in user habits. Traditional consumer banking (prior to automated teller machines—ATMs) was based on a customer's satisfaction with the convenient retail branch. Long-term relationships were often created through friendly, personal service by the local teller. ATMs, with their 24-hour, broader location base, shifted the relationship from service first to convenience first. Similarly, the selection of a bank became more of a commodity-driven convenience (although relationships and reputations continued to factor in the selection of a bank).

Banking on the Internet shifts the relationship even further. Convenience is no longer defined by the closest ATM but by the ability to securely access account information online, to find out about alternative financial service options, and to transfer funds. Or so progressive thinking about the consumer banking industry could assume. Migration of customers from offline account management to online account management is therefore technically viable. But is it intuitively viable from the customer perspective?

The reality is that banking is critically dependent on the customer's expectation that his or her money is in a secure place. For many, this may still conjure up images of a dusty vault in the basement of the local retail branch. Recognizing the efficiency of both cost and convenience, how does a bank drive customer expectations online?

The value proposition of account management may have a greater appeal to a specific subset of customers. Rather than implementing a broad-based strategy, it may be more effective to position the online services to target customers who don't have a preconceived notion of banking via dusty vaults—to build awareness among the young, tech savvy and to grow a market from seed relationships. Unlike the case of the supplier and the customer with preexisting relationships, the opportunity here is not to modify behavior but to create an entirely new level of customer expectations.

The first objective in developing an achievable, results-oriented online strategy is, therefore, to succinctly define the traditional habits of the target user. In the banking example noted above, the target users were defined first as customers but second as specifically those customers that did not have a preexisting relationship with the bank. This focus was strategically based on the assumption that new, young customers would be more likely to bank online. The downside of targeted positioning is potential alienation of other users. In the case of the bank strategy to target young customers, a site that is too hip or out-of-line with the traditional bank image may alienate the core customer base who still may find occasion to visit the site for general banking information. At the other extreme, revealing too much information online may create a competitively disadvantageous strategy.

Managing customer expectations online may mean building a site not around traditional business lines, products, services, support, and so forth, but around lifestyle or targeted-audience needs. Understanding the value of targeted services, Gomez Advisors, in their ongoing ranking of bank sites, uses service to different customer profiles as a primary parameter in ranking bank sites. Through this system, online banking is no longer based on traditional business lines, products, services, and support but on the needs of specific audiences—suppliers, new young customers, new older customers, and existing customers, who conjointly supported by the traditional business lines. Those bank sites with the highest ranking are the ones that meet the expectations of specific target customers.

■ MANAGING CUSTOMER RELATIONSHIPS

Recognizing that customers will have expectations from the web site is the first step in achieving an effective positioning strategy. The next step is determining how to manage those relationships.

Returning to the earlier example, it was concluded that of the potential visitors to the banking site, new, young customers would have a greater long-term return through their online relationships than older customers, who would be less likely to complete their traditional banking transactions online.

For the older customer, the online positioning is not meant to replace the existing relationship but to supplement it, perhaps by providing an online resource for additional information. Older customers may therefore be interested in resources, such as a mortgage calculator with a request form. They may also be interested in comparing the interest rates for the various available accounts. However, they may not be interested in entering personal information online, which they may interpret as a compromise of their own privacy. User friendly tools are alternative options that are doable and that should not be incredibly time-consuming or labor intensive to implement. In this case, the objective is to find a window for a stronger customer relationship but not necessarily a doorway to a new banking relationship.

The young customer, without any predefined conception about banking, may be very receptive to establishing an online relationship. The experience of the young customer may be very different than that of the older customer. For example, the young customer may first want to find out about banking options. By asking a few general questions (Do you currently have a bank account? Do you think you'll need to borrow money in the near future?), the site can begin to capture and create a customized profile of this customer. This information serves the twofold purpose of filtering out unnecessary information (no short-term interest in purchasing a home, therefore mortgage information is not relevant at this time) and creating a disincentive to go to another bank site (as the incentive to reenter the same personal information twice diminishes).

Willingness to provide generic information may very easily translate to providing more specific information given the proper incentives. For example, if the site can smartly recommend that, by entering in a home Zip code and e-mail address, the young customer can receive a customized recommendation for an account set up specifically for him or her, the customer may value this custom information as enough of an incentive to enter this key profile data.

CUSTOMER RELATIONSHIP MANAGEMENT

In developing a tangible value proposition for the end user, it is critical not only to define the first interaction but also to develop an ongoing strategy of customer relationship management.

Recommending an account may logically lead to opening an account, especially if (remembering that this is a technosavvy customer) account information can be accessed online. Positioning this capability as a positive value-added incentive, instead of as a replacement of a traditional (and comfortable) monthly statement, sets the precedent and the expectations for the new customer relationship. Having established this position, the bank has now created a differentiated customer relationship.

■ DEVELOPING CUSTOMER PROFILES

In the two examples outlined, the first requires the delivery of nonintrusive customer information. The second requires a detailed customer management system in which a customer is defined not at the traditional acquisition point but at the initial inquiry point.

Imagine if a retail branch of a bank measured a customer as every individual who walked by the bank on any given day. In reality, the fact that the individual walks by the bank is proof of geographical proximity, which may be a primary motivator for selection of a bank. Yet the ability to track each potential walkby customer is nearly impossible from both a logistic and a technical perspective.

The web site, though, presents a unique opportunity to track the passerby. Through third-party tracking programs, details such as domain address (indicative of company or Internet service provider), length of site visit, and path through the site can immediately fingerprint the passerby.

Returning to the retail bank, a passerby who actually walks into the branch and either picks up some material or meets with a customer representative becomes an even more likely acquisition candidate. Unfortunately, save for the film in the security camera, there is no process in place to track that "almost" customer.

On the web site, that almost customer can receive customized information with just a few keystrokes. As noted earlier, inquiries about the bank account that meets all the needs of the customer can be tracked and logged in exchange for an e-mail and a Zip code. In addition to the tracking application noted for the web site, the infrastructure of the site should now also include a customer database that can record customer inquiries, accept unique data about each customer to create a personal customer record, and batch this data into reports for further internal action.

By the time that the traditional passerby becomes an active customer in the retail branch, the online customer is already an active record in the customer-profiling system. Targeted positioning is enhanced by an architecture that enables immediate development of customized profiles. Bank One, ranked high in early 2000 as a top banking site by Gomez Advisors, focuses on customer service by providing a variety of online tools that target specific customer needs. For example, their free mortgage search tracks the Internet rate of popular search programs, a direct benefit to potential mortgage applicants and a way to track market demand for mortgages prior to the application process.

ONLINE AWARENESS

Creating an online awareness campaign begins with a proactive strategy to first track site usage and to then create incentives, through personalized information, to begin to gather and subsequently customize and differentiate the target customer experience.

■ CREATING CUSTOMER AWARENESS

It can be argued that on the web, with all its benefits of customer tracking and profiling, there is still no way to position a site so that it receives the same visibility as a prominently placed retail branch at the crossroads of the busiest streets in any town or city.

Although the Internet does not create the traditional crossroad, a targeted positioning strategy can pave the way for a focused marketing campaign to generate awareness about the site.

Recall the earlier focus on young, techno-savvy banking customers. This focus naturally generates a marketing strategy.

The first focus of this marketing strategy is to further define the audience demographics and their special online habits. These demographics should include age, gender, lifestyle (student, professional), purchase patterns, and geographic bias (despite the global reach of the Internet, it is sometimes possible to segment based on geography).

After specifically defined the audience demographics, the next step is to assess their online habits. This assessment should take place in the form of both primary and secondary research. Primary research should include not only discussion focus groups and phone interviews but also online focus groups, where surfing habits of the representative group are voluntarily tracked over a set period of time. Secondary research will include reports developed by research groups like Forrester and Jupiter as well as a search for relevant articles.

With the completion of the research phase, the first focus of the marketing strategy will include a detailed customer profile as well as an analysis of the online habits of the target audience.

The second focus of the marketing strategy is to create an online promotional strategy that not only will reach the target audience but also will give them the incentive to visit the site.

Promotional strategies include creating initial visibility through listings in search engines (either free listings or the purchase of keywords based on the audience demographics), advertising on sites trafficked by the target audience, and creating a promotional cross-link program with complementary sites. Online incentive programs to generate traffic to the site may include sponsorship of a popular content section of a complementary site or e-mail newsletter, a game or a survey advertised on other sites with a prize, or "friends and family" or affiliate program, in which referrals receive some sort of bonus when they send someone to the site. For example, Be Free provides the technology to rapidly implement affiliate marketing programs and is just one example of a tool that should be incorporated into the online marketing strategy.

The third focus of the marketing strategy should be crossover programs through traditional offline campaigns. Radio or television spots will help drive customers to the site, as will print advertisements and direct-mail campaigns.

Implementation of a marketing program like this, which implicitly includes ongoing development, will help create awareness and will drive the target audience to the site. Once they are there, the next step is to keep them coming back.

MARKETING TO GENERATE AWARENESS
_____

The awareness campaign should typically include at least three steps:

1. Further differentiation of user online habits through primary and secondary research.
2. Development of an online promotional strategy.
3. Implementation of a crossover marketing program through traditional offline campaigns.

■ SUSTAINING THE CUSTOMER RELATIONSHIP

How many sites does the average person visit on a daily basis? Of those sites, what percentage are sites that have been previously visited and what percentage are new? Although the Internet provides a vast amount of information, there is a relatively small segment of sites that receive significant follow-on visits.

On the Internet, a site should first deliver a compelling experience and then follow up that experience with ongoing, updated content. For example, visiting Yahoo!, one of the most highly trafficked web sites, initially delivers a very straightforward, simple experience for the end user. Enter a word into the search box on the home page, and receive the names of a series of sites that are somehow associated with that word—a very simply concept and, it may be argued, not even that effective because some of the site link results may be broken or irrelevant.

Why, then, do visitors return a second or even a third time to the Yahoo! site? Each time that the visitor returns to the Yahoo! site, she or he may be searching for a different subject. Yahoo! will yield results relevant to that specific search. Even if the search is the same, the results may be different because Yahoo! claims to continually update its site directory.

As the user becomes comfortable with Yahoo!, she or he may notice additional offerings that deliver customized information. My Yahoo! will deliver topic-specific news, portfolio stock quotes, and other highly personalized information. Yahoo! also provides a free e-mail service, which draws the user to the site every time she or he checks for new mail. The use of the "yahoo.com" e-mail address as well as the automatic promotional Yahoo! message at the bottom of each Yahoo!-generated e-mail provides similar reinforcement and promotion of the Yahoo! brand. Even if the user does not use the core search feature of the site each day, the relationship with Yahoo! is sustained through complementary services.

But, it may be argued, Yahoo! is a major brand with significant resources. How can a smaller, niche-oriented site, such as a regional bank, sustain similar relationships?

The first step to sustaining a long-term relationship online is to capture the user. Yahoo! leveraged the core search feature by offering ancillary services that reinforced its image. In a traditional bank, the first stage in the committed relationship is getting the customer to open an account. The next stage, and the first step in sustaining the relationship, is encouraging the customer to complete regular transactions through the account. Offline, this may occur by offering free checks or discounted fees on account transfers. Online, the bank can capture the customer by providing the secure ability to review account information that will support those transactions. Therefore, step one for the bank may be providing access to review account information.

The next step in sustaining an online relationship is incorporating the user into the online experience by allowing her or him to interact with the site. Again, returning to Yahoo!, by providing the capability not only to track but also to update a stock portfolio on the site, Yahoo! is incorporating the user by enabling her or him to publish customized information. Similarly, on the local bank site, whereas allowing the customer to access personal account information delivers a captivating experience, creating the secure mechanism for the customer to transfer funds creates a distinct service that is both convenient and habitual.

The third step in sustaining the online customer relationship is creating a mechanism by which a response is generated, thereby creating a two-way dialogue. In the case of Yahoo!, when a user modifies the tracking stocks, this may trigger a mechanism by which the site automatically offers to track headline news in that stock's industry or to provide a link to the sites of similar companies. The site is programmed to respond to the customized actions of the users. In a similar approach, the bank site may be programmed so that if the customer account runs low on funds, a message is automatically generated offering a personal line of credit (subject to approval). The relationship thus becomes not a one-way dialogue but a two-way conversation customized to the user's need and creating a long-term sustainable relationship.

Sustaining a status quo relationship, however, does not create the incentive to build on the initial needs of the user.

LONG-TERM RELATIONSHIPS

Once the initial relationship has been established, the next step is creating the incentives for habitual use of the site by creating an ongoing user experience.

■ BUILDING THE LONG-TERM CUSTOMER STRATEGIES

Creating a customer relationship that guarantees a nice, steady annuity is certainly a successful positioning strategy. However, building that relationship over time so that the customer commits to additional services or products creates opportunities for long-term growth.

At the retail bank site, the customer is now a steady patron, checking account balances and transferring funds on a nice steady basis. How do you transfer that online checking account customer to an online home mortgage customer? As noted earlier, in sustaining the relationship, the ultimate objective is creating a two-way conversation. Without becoming too intrusive, certain actions on the site should trigger additional actions. Some of these triggers may be automated. For example, if the site incorporates some sort of tracking system in which the user's originating site (that site from which he or she leaves to access the bank site) is reported, this information can be used to better understand the customer's needs. If the customer is frequently linking from a new car directory site, such as Auto-by-tel, to check his or her account balance, this may indicate potential interest in a new car loan.

Alternatively, the bank may want to consider reciprocal programs. The bank may develop a cross-promotional program with a car directory site, for example, perhaps working together to develop a bank-branded listing of new cars. These cross-promotional or affiliate programs help to build the long-term relationship with the customer. As these affiliate programs grow, the bank creates a stronger brand and a deeper relationship with the customer.

Another affiliate relationship may be in the area of bill payment. While providing the capability to pay bills online is useful, the opportunity to check usage history or account details (all at the bank site) can have a dramatic impact on building the relationship. For example, if the customer not only can pay a telephone bill at the bank site but also can review details about individually placed calls, the services provided at the site deepens the relationship with the bank. The value of that service may be increased by working out an arrangement with the telephone company for account review at the point of bill payment. Building the relationship is therefore no longer focused on one unique relationship (that of the customer) but is based on cross-leveraging multiple relationships through the efficiencies generated through the web site.

A positioning strategy on the Internet is created by first understanding the needs of the target audience, then building a two-way relationship based on these needs, and subsequently cross-leveraging resources to strengthen across-the-board relationships that create overall business efficiencies.

LONG-TERM CUSTOMER RELATIONSHIPS

The final step in assessing the marketing conditions that will deliver a successful online strategy is creating an environment to build long-term relationships with the target-user base. This strategy can be achieved by:

1. Understanding customer expectations by defining the unique value that the site will have to the target user.

2. Managing customer relationships by segmenting target-user needs.

3. Developing individual customer profiles and then creating a service strategy based on those specific needs.

4. Creating customer awareness through both an online and an offline marketing strategy.

5. Building a strategy based on long-term retention and not solely on initial acquisition.

Chapter 7

Building the Engine

At this stage in the project planning process, the strategic objectives and milestones have been clearly defined, and the underlying market conditions have been assessed and incorporated into the online strategy. The next step in the development of the project plan is the identification of resources (process requirements, branding, and architecture). This process begins with an outline of those conditions that will impact the site infrastructure. The infrastructure of the web site can be divided into three layers: (1) the user experience, defined by the site schema and the organization of information on the site; (2) the process or middle layer, in which the user takes some action and that action requires some process to generate a reaction; and (3) the functional or core applications layer, in which the data is derived and forwarded back to the end user. Although the user experience is built on the market conditions outlined earlier, the traditional corporate identity often drives the primary design elements of the user experience. Similarly, the core applications layer is usually based on the integration of the site architecture into legacy systems (preexisting internal operating systems).

Using the three-layered framework of the site, the next step in the project blueprint is defining preexisting branding elements and legacy architecture requirements.

BLUEPRINT

After definition of the market conditions, the next stage in the project blueprint is to use the three-layered framework of the site architecture—user experience, process layer, and core applications which will also define the impact of any preexisting design elements and legacy systems.

■ SITE ARCHITECTURE

Modeling the site architecture into a three-layered infrastructure not only provides a framework for the system processes that enable a seamless user experience, but also creates discrete subsets of the resources required to build the site. The user experience layer will require the resources of a design team, while the process layer will require the skills of programmers and developers fluent in Internet protocols. The functional layer will require the skills of engineers and developers adept at working with core applications.

➤ The First Layer—User Experience

The first layer of the web site is the information that is immediately accessible to the target audience. This information may range from static pages of content to content that is updated regularly through a real-time feed of information from another site (such as a news clipping service), to information that is customized to a specific end user based on a user id or on some other profiling technology that calls on the delivery of specific information.

This first layer is also represented through the site schema, an organized flow chart of site content. The schema includes designation of primary site sections and the drill-down, or user progression, through pages of the site. For example, a main objective of the site may be to generate customer leads by establishing the credibility of the company. A primary site section may therefore be to provide regularly updated industry information that positions the site and, subsequently, the company as a de facto industry resource.

In addition to information, this layer also includes the overall look and feel, or identity, of the site—placement of logos, navigational elements, design, and similar identity components of the site. The successful execution of this first layer will deliver a seamless and intuitive experience to the target audience. If well-executed, the target user will then engage or interact with the site through specific site processes.

➤ The Second Layer—Process

Like the first layer that requires customized design and delivery of a unique user experience, the second layer—the process layer—will require the development of customized applications to specifically respond to the actions of the end user. In this layer, the inquiry submitted by the end user is processed and forwarded to the appropriate core application. For example, a user may submit an inquiry for additional information about a specific product. This information may include the user name, company, e-mail address, and specific product. The process systems embedded into the second layer of the site will parse, or segment, this information into discrete fields that can then be distributed to the appropriate core application.

Building on the previous example, suppose a visitor to the site has requested information about a specific product. To find the product, the visitor goes to the site "search" section and enters a "keyword" description of the product. When the visitor enters the term a process is triggered in the middle layer of the site, which reads that request and then calls to a legacy inventory database to search for that keyword in the various products listed in inventory. A select list of products is then generated, once again in the secondary layer (note that there is no change in the core inventory database except for a search function), and a page is generated for posting in the first layer of the site.

The visitor then selects one of the products returned in the generated list and indicates an interest in purchasing the product (often referred to as placing it in a "shopping cart"). This request is processed in the second layer so that a new record in a new database, based on customer profiles, is created (note that there is, as of yet, no impact on the inventory database in which the product was originally forwarded). The response is then to create a new page inquiry (often referred to as "check out") in which a new page is generated (or an existing "check out" template is returned) with open fields for billing, shipping, and transactions data.

The visitor will then enter this data, which is processed in the second layer, as follows:

1. All information is formatted for a customer profile database. This database may be used to track future orders (establishing an account), to provide recommendations for additional orders (an order for a telephone, for example, may trigger a response to recommend the purchase of additional telephone cables), and to create an account id/password so that the new customer will not have to reenter this data during a later purchase

(creating an ease-of-use incentive to discourage future purchases from competitors).

2. Shipping information is forwarded to the shipping company to establish the order and to set up an automated tracking system. Shipping information may also be coordinated with a program generated to calculate taxes.

3. Transaction data may be processed and forwarded to a third-party credit card authentication service, which will then confirm the transfer of funds between the customer and corporate banks, or the data may be forwarded to an accounts receivable application to track and generate an invoice.

So, from the very simple request to purchase a product, there are a series of internal processes that gather the data and distribute it across the appropriate applications as shown in Figure 7.1.

The middle layer subsequently processes the information from the end user, distributes the information in the appropriate format to the core applications, filters the responses or data generated from the core applications, and returns them in a format accessible to the end user.

Processing a customer order is just one example of the integration required in the second layer of the web site architecture. As the data drawn from the end user becomes more complicated, the accompanying processes create an additional level of complexity that must tie into the third layer—core applications.

➤ The Third Layer—Core Applications

The third layer is where the data actually resides. This data may be generated by information delivered through the web

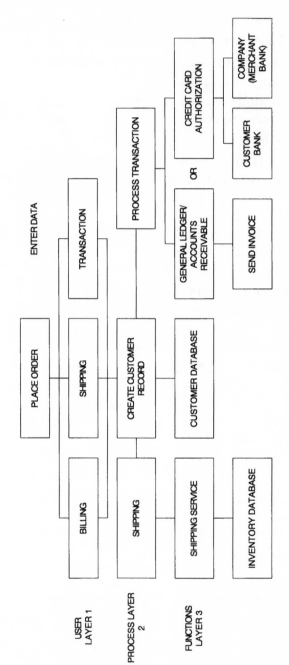

Figure 7.1 Website infrastructure.

site, such as the customer profile information noted earlier. Alternatively, it may be based on data residing in a legacy system. As noted in the previous example, this data could be an inventory system, or it could be access to a third-party shipping or transaction system.

The underlying infrastructure of the core applications may also dictate the overall site architecture. For example, if the inventory system is based on an Oracle database, it may be more cost-effective to build the process layer into an integrated database format than to introduce a third-party infrastructure.

The frequency of the processing will also have an impact on the site infrastructure. Whereas one architecture may be well suited for a few, highly secure transactions at any given time, another architecture may be better equipped to handle a high volume of smaller transactions. It is therefore critical to define what is often referred to as the "anticipated site throughput" when determining the site architecture.

As noted earlier, there are two preexisting, or legacy, elements that will have a primary impact on the development of the three-layered site infrastructure. The first legacy is the preexisting corporate identity or market brand. The second legacy is the preexisting system architecture. As further detailed later, both will have a significant impact on the seamless execution of the site strategy.

FROM BRANDING TO SYSTEM ARCHITECTURE

With definition of the site process, the next step is to define any preexisting variables that will impact the seamless launch of the site strategy. These variables range from branding to system architecture.

■ BRANDING OF THE WEB SITE

Because of the international reach of the Internet, the brand and particularly the names selected to represent it can have far-reaching implications. Furthermore, in a market in which significant track records are measured barely in years, the positioning of the brand can have a fundamental impact on the success of the strategy. Full-scale site branding should therefore include an assessment of online naming strategies and definition of key visual elements.

➤ Online Naming Strategies

In the online battle of the cola, who do you think wins the "dot" naming challenge? While Pepsi owns pepsi.com, pepsiworld.com, and pepsico.com, but it does not own pepsi.net. Nor, as it is noted at pepsi.net, does the corporation own pepsibloodbath.com, a site formerly protesting bullfight advertising by Pepsi. Also, Pepsi does not own pepsi.org. That address is owned by Public Existentialist Programs for Surrealistic Imaginations. On the other hand, Coca-Cola owns coke.com, coke.net, and coke.org. But who owns cola.com? That address is not owned by Pepsi. In fact, it is not even owned by Coca-Cola. Rather, it is owned by Cola.com, Inc., a company based in Colorado (with a simple "under construction" web site).

So, when developing an online branding strategy, the first step is to consider the site name. According to Network Solutions, an online service to register domain names, a new domain address is registered every five seconds.

A brand is created to establish an emotional connection between a product or service and the need that it fulfills. The brand "Ivory" may now be equated with cleanliness and purity because Ivory is "99 44/100% pure." However, the term "ivory" has many different meanings. Ivory could be a color (slightly off white), or it could be part of an animal (check out those ivory tusks) or part of a musical instrument (tickle the ivories and let's hear some tunes). Ivory could mean one thing in English but something else in Japanese. Its English characters have no meaning to a Chinese student, yet its use as a soap may still be relevant. In fact, ivory.com is owned by Procter & Gamble, while ivory.net is owned by an organization based in Italy, and Ivory.org is owned by an individual with the last name Ivory.

When naming standards were established for the Internet, almost anyone could register a domain address, that is, a web site name, followed by a top-level suffix (e.g., .com for business or .edu for an academic institution). Little thought was given to the international or, for that matter, national conflicts that might arise. Yet a domain address truly becomes an immediate international brand because anyone with access to the Internet may try to reach it.

This international branding is truly wonderful if it is that unique brand that no one else can claim. But what if Delta Airlines would like to register delta.com? After all, they do have rights to the term "delta," especially as it applies to an airline. But what about Delta Dental or Delta Computers or the myriad of other Delta companies that exist? Do they all have equal claim to "delta," or does size and reputation enable one company to take precedent over the other?

On the Internet, usage generally dictates rights to a name unless, of course, the only use of the name is to hold it hostage until the other company purchases it. Lawsuits have been fought and won over historical precedent that dictates rights to a name. Branding on the Internet truly internationalizes trade names and sets all new precedents for usage and rights associated with a trademarked name. Yet, it all begins with the historical usage of the name that creates the brand.

Legacy of the Name

A brand creates a legacy reputation for a company or a product. A popular brand may conjure up positive memories just as a one-time negative experience can forever taint a brand.

A brand may be at the corporate level, Procter & Gamble (P&G), or at the product level, Tide, or even at a subproduct level, fragrance-free Tide.

Or, so the theory goes. In reality, companies may register all domain names at every top level to protect their brand. As Pepsi may have recognized in the registered use of the web site pepsibloodbath.com, it is unfortunate for an online user to find a corporate name affiliated with a negative propaganda piece.

At the same time, countries have their own dedicated suffix. For example, ".ie" is affiliated with Ireland, while ".jp" is associated with Japan. Whether a company should register individual domain addresses across every suffix depends on the market reach of the company. If the company does have an international presence, it should consider registering in multiple countries if for no other reason than to prevent another entity from compromising the brand by posting unfavorable information.

Then, there is the question of translation. Is it necessary to register the French or the Japanese version of the name at the same time? Again, this depends on the reach of the brand, but it may be considered as part of the strategy.

Finally, there is the mixing of the name with a prefix or, occasionally, a suffix. For example, should P&G register tide.com, thetide.com, and tidedetergent.com? What about tide-detergent.com? As of early 2000, both tidedetergent.com and tide-detergent.com were still available for registration.

The cost to register a domain address is trivial. However, figuring out and maintaining all the possible configurations of a brand can become a full-time job. So, some degree of restraint in registering domain names is advised, as well as the understanding that legal recourse for defamation of character brand does have some precedent on the Internet.

Experience and Expressions

There are also generic names or expressions that can imply a certain brand. For example, when searching for Tide, a user may first type in www.detergent.com (not owned by P&G). In the actual case of Procter & Gamble's Tide, the company has registered clothesline.com, to capture not only a specific product but also an experience.

HP Hood, a New England dairy, created an advertising campaign around a Mom who answered questions about dairy products. For this campaign, Hood created a separate domain address, www.hoodanswermom.com, which then tied into the main site, www.hphood.com.

NAMING STRATEGIES

A well-defined naming strategy is a key element of the overall branding strategy. This strategy should include both derivatives and extensions of the product and/or corporate name as well as global naming practices.

Visual Image and Expectations

Brand is also consistent with a visual image. The expectation for the visual experience on the Arm & Hammer Baking Soda web site, for example, is very different from the visual experience expected from the MTV web site.

As a hip, relatively new medium, the Internet can be an opportunity to expand or to refresh a brand. However, the Internet is not the place to create a new logo or an icon that is nothing like the traditional image. Remember that users are typing in "Heinz" or "Nabisco" with a predefined expectation of a brand.

A complex product or service may not readily transfer to the web. Although both audio and video are technically available through the Internet, many users currently do not have either the tolerance or the computer capability for viewing information in this way. In 2000, the Internet offers a highly interactive experience ("click here for more information") that can lead to a two-way exchange but does not offer the fluidity of message supported by the audiovisual experience of television or the audio experience of radio. Therefore, the Internet requires its own unique iteration of the brand. A promotion reinforcing the brand may run consistently across all mass media, but it must be adapted for the strength of each one. For example, the print ad may include a beautiful, high-resolution image; the radio ad may include two people conversing about the image whereas the television ad may include some action or movement to support the dialogue of the radio. The web site may contain a static image that, when the user moves the cursor over it, changes to review some product details or a particular message invoking additional action. Thus, a brand image is adjusted slightly to each medium as a sensory experience. The web is no exception, with the primary experience at this stage being both visual and tactile.

Large corporations often have a predefined set of corporate design specifications or a corporate style sheet that includes use and application of the logo and other corporate design elements, a corporate typeface, and a prespecified color palette. Although these elements may not be relevant to the web site in every case, they should still be defined within the site blueprint for reference by the design team in the development of the site interface.

BLUEPRINT

Design of the web site will be fundamentally impacted by preexisting corporate design specifications, including logos, typefaces, and palette. These specifications should be clearly defined within the site blueprint as a series of standards or guidelines for the development of the overall site interface.

■ LEGACY OF THE ARCHITECTURE

At the other extreme of legacy integration is the impact of existing system architecture. If the greatest advantage of the Internet idea is to process thousands of daily transactions, yet the existing highly complex internal system cannot process these transactions, then the strategy is doomed to failure.

Depending on the specific online application, the legacy system may include an inventory system, a financial system, or even a manufacturing system. As noted earlier, taking orders online may be a highly efficient online business objective; however, if it is not integrated into the back-end inventory system, it may ultimately create a backlog in orders and dissatisfied customers.

Development of the online system should begin with carefully defined specifications of the existing legacy systems. In turn, these specifications may define the online system architecture that will have an impact on both the functional and the user experience layers of the site development. Adaptation of the legacy architecture for web-based integration may also require the involvement of an engineering team that is fluent in that specific system.

Another consideration is the hosting and the access strategies (including hardware specifications) that will be defined by projected use and site processing. A systemwide crash or downtime (as happened with eBay in 1999 because systems were not built to support the number of users that simultaneously accessed the site information) can shake the confidence of even the most loyal user. Tampering or infiltration of a supposedly secure Internet transaction process (as happened with a major search engine service) can quickly diminish the reputation of a corporation's ability to do business. Definition of firewall and security systems are, therefore, a critical element in the successful launch of the site.

Finally, the development of an integrated only system will usually require the cooperation of the internal information

BLUEPRINT

Definition of legacy architecture in the site blueprint is critical to the seamless execution of an online strategy. Prespecified elements should include: definition of legacy systems, preferences for site architecture, hosting and access (including projected scale requirements), definitions of firewall and security systems, the roles and responsibilities of the internal and the external development teams, and requirements for ongoing maintenance (including training).

technology (IT) staff. Within the site blueprint, it is therefore critical to define the roles and responsibilities of both the internal team and the external vendor team. As discussed in greater detail in Chapter 12, these definitions will also have an impact on the ongoing maintenance requirements (including staffing and training).

➤ Application Service Providers

When building a long-term online strategy, careful consideration should also be given to the internal versus the external development of the site architecture. Because the architecture of the Internet is still evolving, investments in software and hardware may become functionally obsolete long before the end of the amortization schedule. Therefore, there has been a fundamental shift in the bottom-line valuation of an Internet-based strategic investment.

Where traditional accounting took into effect the value of expenditures in software and hardware, the emerging financial model for Internet strategies also takes into account the value of the information processed through those investments. Because the underlying architecture is still evolving, the new model of expenditure is to license core technologies from pureplay application service providers and lease space on servers maintained by third-party vendors, but to retain all rights to the information that is generated through the licensed software. For example, a company may decide to pursue a more efficient procurement process through an exchange auction. Bids are solicited on an as-needed basis, and suppliers respond accordingly. Whereas the traditional processing constraints limited the pool of prospective supplies, the efficiencies gained through a standardized auction process will enable more potential vendors to submit others.

> ### APPLICATION SERVICE PROVIDERS
>
> With the ongoing rapid evolution of the Internet-based systems, it may be more appropriate to license core applications from a third-party developer, also known as an application service provider, than to build the system from scratch internally.

To develop this new procurement process, the Internet manager has two alternatives. In developing an integrated solution, the Internet manager must first decide if it is more efficient to develop the technology in-house or license it from a third-party application service provider. The benefit of developing the technology in-house is control and access to the core applications. However, given the rapid pace of Internet development, the Internet manager may be better off licensing the technology from an application service provider responsible for maintaining and updating the system application. With this alternative, the corporate asset is the information that flows through the system but not the technology itself. In the case of the new procurement system, the company can take every advantage of an online bid and solicitation process without the added cost of maintaining the core system.

IDENTIFICATION OF RESOURCES

The first step in actually executing the business strategies outlined in the site blueprint is defining those elements that are tied into preexisting corporate operations. Branding strategies range from naming conventions to visual elements such as a logo or a corporate typeface. Architecture design includes preexisting systems that will be tied in to the strategic decision of ownership rights in regard to customized application development.

1. The site processes can be defined in terms of three layers: (1) the user experience, (2) the process, and (3) the functional specifications tied in to the preexisting legacy systems.

2. Legacy systems include the brand and the corporate identity and extend to online naming conventions.

3. System architecture is dependent on clearly defined specifications for legacy systems.

4. Careful definition of roles and responsibilities in the integration of legacy systems is required to ensure the seamless execution of the online strategy.

5. An up-front business decision should be made about licensing preexisting applications versus building from scratch and owning all rights to the online system architecture.

Part III
Identification of
Resources

Chapter 8

Writing the Directions

After using the three-layered architecture to define the site processes, the next step in the identification of resources is the development of the *request for proposal* (RFP). Whereas the project plan is an internal document that defines the business guidelines, the RFP is a *public* or commercial document that is used to assess and select the external resources that will be used to execute the site blueprint. It should parallel the project blueprint but should provide only the information that is relevant to the specific tasks assigned to the outside vendors.

■ THE REQUEST FOR PROPOSAL

Like the project blueprint, the RFP includes six sections:

1. Definition of the strategic statement.
2. Outline of the market conditions.
3. Branding and design specifications.

4. System architecture.

5. Vendor requirements.

6. Time line and budget.

BLUEPRINT

The RFP is the public version of the site blueprint and is used to solicit and select the external resources that will be hired to deliver the site specifications. Like the blueprint, it should include six sections:

1. Definition of the strategic statement.

2. Outline of the market conditions.

3. Branding and design specifications.

4. System architecture.

5. Vendor requirements.

6. A time line and a budget.

Because a launch can draw on so many unique resources, an RFP should serve to define not only the deliverables but also the service that each resource will provide. One of the greatest challenges in delivering a site on time and on budget is making sure at the start of the project that appropriate resources are available and allocated. *Project creep* (development extending beyond the initial scope and, usually, budget), which is endemic to the Internet industry, is primarily due to the open-ended expectations that lead to ambiguous specifications and poorly defined deliverables. The cure for project creep is the deliverables defined in the RFP.

The RFP serves as the groundpoint for the technical specifications—the finitely defined deliverables of the third-party resources. The primary difference among the project blueprint, the RFP, and the technical specifications is the target audience. The project blueprint is for the internal project management team; the RFP is for soliciting vendors; the technical specifications are for the development team.

The RFP is a general document that defines the project and the resource requirements of third-party vendors. It is purposely generic because, as a public bid, despite the best efforts of everyone involved, it could be reviewed by a competitive team, or it could serve to define a unique market opportunity for a vendor to develop independent of the project. An RFP should generally be considered a document for the public domain.

The use and the audience for the various documents that are required to launch a successful online strategy are summarized in the following chart:

Document	Author	Audience	Purpose
Blueprint	Project manager	Internal review only	Definition of corporate objectives, market conditions, and development strategies
RFP	Project Manager and internal development team	Internal and development partners	Definition, solicitation, and selection of third party resources
Technical specifications	Development partners	Development team (both internal and external)	Specifications of site deliverables

■ SECTION 1: DEFINITION OF THE STRATEGIC STATEMENT

The first section of the RFP should summarize the Internet objectives and place them in the context of emerging industry trends. As the introduction of the project to the third-party vendors, it should also provide some background information about the company and its ability to execute the business objectives. As exemplified, this section should do the following:

➤ *Define the industry.* In the case of a reseller of parts to manufacture business equipment, the industry definition may include the number of traditional distributors, the size of the market, the company's regional versus international presence, and a brief history of the submitting company's background and experience in the industry.

➤ *Summarize the traditional business process.* Extrapolated from the project blueprint, this section should succinctly define the key factors that limit the traditional business process. For the parts reseller, it may be a simple statement that the traditional business process includes three to seven resellers with each receiving a commission of 1.5 percent to 3 percent of each sale. Also, distribution may lag because parts are shipped from a single facility through a single contracted shipper.

➤ *Outline the online business process.* Although the project blueprint will outline the online business process in greater detail, the RFP will provide some guidelines to consider in qualifying the vendor opportunity. For example, the parts reseller may include the opportunity to decrease the number of resellers and to increase overall margins to the remaining resellers. It may also provide an alternative solution to the traditional logistics bottleneck of a central distribution facility through a real-time inventory network of strategically positioned distributors, which will cut both carry costs and shipping costs.

➤ *Define the site efficiencies to be achieved.* In this section, the internal business objectives are replaced by a review of proposed end-user efficiencies. These efficiencies may include the ability to access account information at any time or the automation of parts reordering through a tie-in to end-user inventory systems.

➤ *Define the business objectives.* Given the external market conditions and the proposed efficiencies for the end user, the overall business objectives of the site are now summarized. For the parts reseller, the business objective may be to shift 30 percent of the existing client base to an integrated online procurement process in six to nine months postlaunch. Alternatively, it may be to acquire a set number of smaller resellers and to generate new business by shifting their preexisting customers online in six to nine months.

➤ *Define the metrics to measure the results.* The metrics to measure the results include concrete milestones, such as "Register three dozen potential customers in the first 30 days postlaunch" or "Process $3 million in orders within the first 90 days postlaunch." Concrete metrics will help set the current architecture for the site and define future scalability.

After defining the overall business landscape for the site, the next step is to specifically define the needs of the target audiences and the current state of the competitive marketplace. These steps are succinctly defined in the second section.

■ SECTION 2: OUTLINE OF THE MARKET CONDITIONS

From the project blueprint, this section will summarize current online market conditions as they specifically pertain to the developing site.

➤ *Define the target user.* The target user for the parts reseller may be current customers, who generate in excess of $5 million in sales each year. These customers may be the end user or another reseller. Interviews and focus groups completed by the reseller before the solicitation of the RFP should indicate online usage habits (including access to the Internet), online transaction usage history, and possibly some information about current inventory tracking systems (for future integration).

➤ *Create a user chart that defines the roles and responsibilities of the primary users.* Because of the number of users involved in the seamless execution of a site (including suppliers, employees, and customers), a user chart will define the specific roles and subsequent needs of each user. Clear definition of the roles of each user will aid in the development and the delivery of a site that will actually meet the projected online objectives.

➤ *Summarize the demographic and psychographic profile of the target user.* Variables such as site access (home use versus office use, for example) will have a fundamental impact on the site architecture. Development of a site with integrated video will not effectively reach a target audience with low bandwidth access to the Internet because of the time required to download that video.

➤ *Create a competitive positioning strategy.* Understanding existing competitive conditions, both online and offline, will enable the site to deliver an offensive rather than a defensive user experience. An offensive strategy is particularly important in the rapidly evolving online market.

➤ *Prioritize the primary competitive variables.* Competing on price may have a very different impact on the user experience than competing on service. Prioritizing and then executing on a strategy that clearly positions the site within a specific market sector will help to ensure its overall viability.

➤ *List both the horizontal and the vertical competitors.* Horizontal competitors are those companies that traditionally compete for market share, while vertical competitors are suppliers and end users that become inherent competitors online because of their ability to go direct and to potentially cut out the intermediary role that a company may play.

➤ *Summarize both the strengths and the weakness of the competition online.* This summary is critical not only because it helps to position the new site in the marketplace but also because it provides a snapshot of existing technologies that may be acquired or licensed as a core application or reverse engineered for fine-tuned development. In this section, it is therefore important to summarize both the strengths and the weaknesses of the competition from the perspectives of design, content, and functionality.

➤ *Create a competitive positioning chart.* This chart will succinctly define the market opportunity based on the fundamental variables that impact the target user's experience.

➤ *Summarize the user expectations.* Understanding the market conditions, it is critical to define the site experience based on the expectations of the target user. Because the goal of the site is usually to change user habits in some way, expectations must be met early on in the acquisition process to ensure a long-term online relationship.

➤ *Define the value proposition.* Site users must have a clearly defined benefit or value in visiting the site, or they won't use it. By defining the value proposition in the RFP, both the internal and the external team will understand the user need and not just the business strategy.

➤ *Target key marketing strategies.* Launch of the site is only the first step in achieving the overall business objectives. The ongoing strategy should include a predefined marketing plan, which may require additional outside services such as an advertising agency.

➤ *Develop a retention strategy.* Building a marketing strategy to entice users to the site once is not enough. Part of the marketing strategy, which, again, may require specific external expertise, is to develop an ongoing strategy to deliver fresh information that will entice the target user to access the site on a regular basis.

■ SECTION 3: BRANDING AND DESIGN SPECIFICATIONS

Legacy of the brand will set the parameters of user expectations on the web site. This legacy will subsequently define the design of the site, ranging from use of industry buzzwords as primary navigational elements to the primary color palette of the site.

➤ *Define naming conventions and/or naming strategies.* Because of the primary role that a web address plays in site usage, a strong naming strategy, including assessment of potential competitive addresses, is an important part of the design and branding strategy.

➤ *Define the existing corporate identity.* If the corporation has an existing style sheet, this is the time to drag it out of storage, dust it off, and note the indisputable rules and regulations that define the existing corporate identity. This may range from proportion of the corporate logo to the corporate name to the name of the illustrator of record for the company (who may become a key partner contact in the design of the site). At minimum, this section will set expectations for the creative liberties to be taken with the site. It should also include definition and perhaps a sample of the logo and the color palette (which could need to be modified to be web-safe for consistent viewing on the web). It may also include definition of the corporate typeface and limitations on usage rights, if any.

➤ *Define and/or attach samples of offline marketing material.* If existing materials are part of the RFP, the vendor will have tangible evidence not only of the traditional look and feel of the corporate identity but also of the tone of the copy and the messages conveyed to the end user. Finally, if there is to be any coordination with an outside advertising agency, contact information may be helpful as the third-party vendors concretely define their roles, resources, and working relationships with the rest of the team.

■ SECTION 4: SYSTEM ARCHITECTURE

Legacy systems may define the infrastructure of the online strategy. Familiarity, experience, and capabilities to adapt this legacy architecture may become the primary factor that defines the on time, on budget launch of the site. Careful documentation or citation of the existing system configuration (noting that this document may be considered as public domain and accessible to either existing or potential competitors) will set the groundwork for delivering an achievable, scalable online strategy.

> ➤ *Define legacy systems.* As much as is appropriate, specifications of hardware and software will help set expectations as well as budgets for the delivery of integration development at the third level of core applications for the site. Consideration should also be given to current usage, potential limitations in scale, and future use. For example, a paper-based invoice system may not be adaptable for long-term integration into an electronic funds-transfer payment system. In the long run, key-entered solutions may prove the efficiency of full-scale replacement of the legacy system.

> ➤ *Define preferences for system architecture as is appropriate.* Preexisting vendor relationships, either at the

hardware or the software level, while not implicit in legacy systems, may impact the development of the site architecture. For example, a long-term commitment to an IBM system architecture may translate into a set of hardware requirements for the site.

➤ *Define hosting and access strategies (include hardware specifications).* Will the site be hosted and maintained in house, or should it be outsourced to a third party? The former option will have an implication on allocation of internal resources, whereas the latter may have an impact on ongoing licensing agreements and upgrades. With the architecture of the Internet still rapidly evolving, outsourcing may minimize risk of site obsolescence, but it may also have a significant impact on overall site cost.

➤ *Define internal resources and processes as they will impact web site development.* Once again, if the existing internal information technology (IT) team will be responsible for system integration, this will have a fundamental impact on the services provided by the third-party vendor. Also, if it is anticipated that an internal team will be hired to maintain the site post-launch, this will have a significant impact on the role of the third-party vendors.

➤ *Define firewall and security systems.* Halfway through the development is not the time to discover that the current configuration (and policy) of access to accounts payable will prevent the delivery of an integrated, online, bill-payment system. Careful research and definition up front will limit these costly mistakes midway through the process.

➤ *Define ongoing maintenance requirements (including training).* Documentation, manuals, training, and ongoing support may be the biggest hidden cost of

site development. Clearly defining expectations re-
garding the ability to modify the site, warranties,
support (round-the-clock [24/7] or 9-to-5), and training should be carefully defined up front to minimize
the impact of the "not my problem" syndrome after
the site is launched.

■ SECTION 5: VENDOR REQUIREMENTS

This section, to be filled out by the vendor, will validate the
qualifications, capabilities, and experience of the prospective vendors. This section should include:

1. *Project team*—typical size and capabilities as well as
   brief biographies on the key team personnel.
2. *Project management process*—a succinct description of
   procedures and policies in regard to project deliverables.
3. *Partnerships and alliances*—preexisting vendor relationships that may impact cite development.
4. *Experience and capabilities*—summaries of similar
   projects as well as specific industry experience.
5. *References*—contact information for prior projects.

■ SECTION 6: TIME LINE AND BUDGET

As much as possible, be up front about the time line and the
budget. If the budget depends on the proposed deliverables,
define expectations in regard to the deadlines for delivery.
Otherwise, the development process may become longer
than originally expected.

➤ *Define project schedule.* The project schedule is driven from two sets of deliverables: (1) the deliverables of the vendor and (2) the deliverables of the company. State realistic expectations for the review-and-approval process up front so that the vendors can incorporate these expectations into their deliverables. Even in the best of all circumstances, it is not unusual for the schedule to slide, so some slippage should also be built into the up-front expectations.

If there are hard deadlines, such as industry cycles (e.g., sales during the holiday season), state these deadlines up front, and be prepared to work as a team to meet them.

➤ *List contact information and response deadline.* Building a team contact list early in the process will help set responsibilities early on and will minimize confusion at a later date. When soliciting the RFP, it is also important to include a contact name for more information and the deadline for submission.

➤ *Define budget preferences (fixed fee versus time and materials).* Again, defining this up front will minimize confusion and misrepresentation at a later date. Details about rates and line items delivered by the submitting vendors will also provide parameters for comparison of vendor deliverables.

With a well-documented RFP, vendors will be able to deliver a tighter response, which in turn can lead to a better-defined and -delivered launch.

■ THE PROCESS

Once the RFP is forwarded, there should be a clearly defined deadline by which to respond. Depending on the scope of the project, this time frame will typically be weeks (not months) in length and should allow time for inquiries and response to the soliciting company.

The submission of the RFP should be accompanied by a formal presentation of services and introduction of key members of the team. Although, if possible, this generally takes place at the offices of the soliciting company, a site visit to the prospective vendor can help qualify not only capabilities but also the character of the potential vendor.

There should then be a reasonable time for internal review (again, weeks rather than months), and all vendors should be notified of final selection. It is also courteous to share feedback with nonselected vendors about their relative strengths and weaknesses.

From selection, the process then goes into negotiation of contract terms, with the first delivery being response to detailed specifications and finitely defined project deliverables.

In summary, this chapter reviewed the process of vendor selection through the solicitation of a request for proposal (RFP)—a summary of the project blueprint to create achievable technical specifications from the vendor partner.

VENDOR SELECTION PROCESS

Key Sections of the RFP:

1. Definition of the Strategic Statement—succinct definition of the business goals.

2. Outline of the Market Conditions—description of the target audience, competitive marketplace, and user experience.

(Continued)

3. Branding and Design Specifications—summary of corporate identity and design style sheet.

4. System Architecture—analysis of the legacy system, hardware, software, and access requirements.

5. Vendor Requirements—experience and capabilities of the soliciting vendors.

6. Time Line and Budget—realistic parameters for the time line and budget.

Chapter 9

Finding the Mechanics

The second stage of the identification of resources is actually finding the vendors that will deliver the best solution given the specifications as outlined. With the explosion of the Internet, thousands of companies now claim some degree of Internet expertise. From all this vast experience, how does the Internet manager solicit, select, and contract the team that is going to best deliver the web site strategy?

Solicitation and selection of vendors can be completed in four steps:

1. Develop a shortlist of potential candidates. The selection of these candidates may be based on prior experience, depth of internal resources, or cost structure.

2. Qualify these skills based on the needs outlined in the project blueprint.

3. Confirm that the vendor resources match the needs of the project, typically through definition of the project team.

4. Review the vendor process for the delivery of the specifications as outlined. This review should include both the submission of a detailed proposal and a presentation by the vendor team.

BLUEPRINT

The third section of the project blueprint will initially include proposals submitted by a preselected group of vendors. Once the proposals have been reviewed, this section will be replaced with the final project scope to be delivered by each vendor. This section typically includes: definition of the project team (resources, skills, experience), their project management process (with reference to prior projects), partnerships and alliances, experience and capabilities (with specific reference to the resources to be assigned to this project), and, finally, vendor references.

Reviewing the specifications developed in Chapter 8, the Internet manager has already begun the first step: prioritizing the business needs of the web site. The next step is to go back to the Internet and, with a critical eye, review those web sites that deliver experiences most similar to the anticipated business site. Unlike the competitive analysis, in which sites are analyzed purely from a competitive perspective, this review should assess the broader context of the user experience. For example, a local newspaper may want to create an online version of its editorial content. For context, it may review other local newspaper sites, not to view the competition, but to assess the style, layout, and resources delivered within those sites. The newspaper may also want to review the top news-oriented sites on the web as well as local community portals to assess alternative resources for information.

The selection of comparison sites should range from the logical ("this site is a clear innovator in this industry") to the emotional ("this site is fun and interesting"). As outlined in

Site	Why Chosen	Type of Site	Appealing Features	Developer

Figure 9.1   Competitive site features.

the above illustration, Figure 9.1, begin to create a list high-lighting what is both appealing and unappealing about these sites.

Once the list includes 8 to 12 sites, take a step back and note if there are any trends. Do the sites have a common look? Do they all offer a specific functionality?

■ CANDIDATE ASSESSMENT

Now, the sleuthing begins. In the stampede to become the Internet resource of choice, Internet companies are seldom shy about listing their successes. These successes will be pro-moted via press releases, in online portfolios, through recog-nition by industry awards or rankings, or, occasionally, through a site credit line. Finding the credit line on a client site is the easiest path to the Internet resources. If listed, this credit is most often found on the homepage (generally near the bottom), on the contact page, or, occasionally, on a site credit page. The credit may also be embedded in the source code. Another alternative is to call the client company di-rectly. Generally, the marketing department will know who built the site. Sometimes, the answer may be, "We built it ourselves." Depending on the site and the internal resources of the company, especially if it is 100 percent Internet based, they may have the resources on payroll, sometimes with the help of a few select freelancers.

In recognition of the best and the brightest in the industry, many associations and industry publishers now sponsor events that give credit to those industry innovators. Often, this recognition is given for a particularly innovative project. For example, if the favorite sites are nationally recognized brands that may have a well-executed design identity, *Adweek* may have carried an article about the interactive team behind the brand. Back issues may be available in print or online. In addition to the recognition of what is, in their opinion, a well-executed strategy, *Adweek* annually ranks the top interactive agencies. Thus, both industry recognition and articles may also provide information about potential vendors.

Given the impact of the Internet on almost every industry sector, most trade publications now devote an occasional feature or even a regular section to important Internet-based industry innovations. Searching through back issues may provide clues about who are the industry's Internet vendors of choice.

Another resource for these services may be industry colleagues. Ask colleagues about vendors with whom they have worked in the past, and visit the sites of their preferred vendors. Once again, with the need to establish capability, vendors are seldom shy about featuring their successes.

In this expedition to find the best and the brightest, this simple sleuthing should narrow the field of prospective vendors. The next step is to determine which vendors have the capabilities to deliver.

■ THE QUALIFYING FACTORS

Services vary from highly specialized one-source shops to full-service firms. A quick examination of their client list provides only so much information, so it may not be indicative of what services the vendor specifically delivers. The next step in qualifying a vendor is to determine how long the company members have been working together, the background of their key personnel, the number of full-time employees (in a fast-growth industry such as this, companies will often manage project swell with the assistance of a few key freelancers), the size of a typical project team and/or project, and their long-term interests.

A relatively young (in the Internet space, this would be anything less than two years) company may be advantageous for a smaller project because it is a new company anxious to grow through project opportunity. However, youth (and inexperience) may be disadvantageous for a larger project. Size of project is determined not only by budget but also by complexity. A young boutique of multimedia specialists may be very appropriate for the design of that segment of the project, but don't assume that they will be able to carry more of the project (even if they assure you otherwise).

Consolidation should not be misinterpreted as youth. Just as a supporting cast of steady freelancers may enhance the core competencies of a boutique, a national network of newly merged corporations may solidify the local talent. With merger, acquisition, divestiture, and start-up the norm in a rapid-growth industry, the key consideration in measuring "age" as a qualifier of experience is to carefully question the track record of the team and their ability to jointly deliver. Of course, this still significantly depends on the scope of the project. As the project demands become more complex, the Internet manager will want to be sure that the full range of services can be delivered. A simple test is to question the prospective vendor about the proposed team structure, including the actual number of people on a typical team. Then, find out how many projects the team undertakes at any given time. Finally, find out how many people are on staff full time,

---

VENDOR TEAMS

In a fast-growth industry, rapid consolidation and the emergence of new companies makes it difficult to determine which vendor provides the best resources at any given time. Qualifiers to judge the ability of a vendor to deliver should therefore be weighted by the size of the company based on the number of employees as compared to the average size of a project team. If a company has 12 employees and an average project team consists of 6 members, then they can only work on a handful of projects at any given time. Conversely, if a company has 120 employees, then there are many more resources available; but, depending on the specific project scope, there may be different levels of skills and experiences that would lower the likelihood of access to the top talent.

---

and assess the pros and cons of being the largest project, drawing on the most resources, or the smallest project, possibly being relegated to the most junior staff.

➤ The Project Team

Whenever possible, it is most helpful to meet and interview the key personnel who will be assigned to the project (and not just the sales team). Although they may simply oversee the delivery of services by junior staff members, it is still important for both sides of the team to understand who will be responsible for the key project components. As demonstrated in Figure 9.2, a web project typically requires the

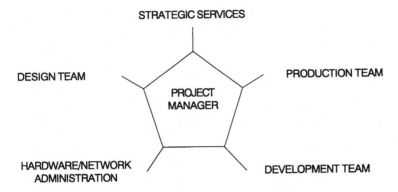

Figure 9.2 Web project team.

skills of a design team, a development team, a production team, as well as the project management team. It may also include the services of a strategic services team to assist in the development of the overall business objectives. These teams may expand or contract depending on the scope of the project.

Design Team

The design team is usually lead by the *creative director*. This person is responsible for working directly with the project manager to develop an overall creative solution and strategy, addressing the needs of the client according to the design objectives.

The *art director* creates a visual interpretation of the creative director's ideas. He or she will design the overall look and feel of the site from a visual perspective.

Occasionally working as part of the design team or hired from an outside resource, the *copywriter* works with the art director to create headlines, copy, and other content suitable to the medium and to the overall strategic objectives.

Development Team

The development team is usually lead by the *interactive director,* sometimes recognized as the web master. Working with the creative director but reporting to the project manager or the account director, the interactive director acts as a coordinator of the project at the technical level. The interactive director must be able to interpret the creative vision in a technical way by identifying the tools and the technical skills that are necessary to implement the project. The interactive director is also the point person for quality assurance processes.

Also reporting to the interactive director, the *web programmer* develops back-end systems and server-side scripting to create additional functionality and interactivity and is generally responsible for any necessary system integration. He or she should be familiar with popular tools used for back-end development and engineering.

The *site engineers* are then responsible for integrating the legacy system into the site functionality. The site engineers should be accredited developers of those legacy systems.

The *network administrator* is responsible for integrating the chosen software applications over the appropriate hardware platform. Reporting to the interactive director, the network administrator is also familiar with the connectivity and access requirements.

The *quality assurance coordinator* tests the system for reliability and accessibility under various conditions and on various platforms. For example, the quality assurance coordinator may test for the time it takes to download an image or if a site performs consistently across various browsers.

The quality assurance coordinator typically reports to the interactive director.

Depending on the scope of the project, a highly specialized *multimedia artist* may also be part of the development team. He or she is responsible for developing any other interactive or multimedia aspects of a project, including media involving animation, sound, or video.

Production Team

The production team may report to either the creative director or the interactive director. If the project is design focused, then the production team will typically include *graphic designers* and *production artists.* If the project is development focused, then the production team may also include *system integrators.* Members of the technical development team will also be familiar with the system application and server-side scripts developed by the web programmer.

Once the project is launched, there may be postproduction training and management. Resources may be drawn from the core project team or may include managers proficient in training and site administration skills.

Project Management Team

The *account director/project manager* manages the client relationships at a senior level. He or she formulates and oversees implementation of interactive strategies consistent with overall business and marketing strategies. The account director leads and motivates the internal account team and manages the account specific profit and loss (P&L) statement.

The *account manager/producer* works with the account director and acts as the team liaison. He or she manages the product schedules, budgets, estimates, and internal accounting/billing. He or she is also responsible for providing written documentation of project strategy, budget, and time line.

Strategic Services Team

The role of strategic services is to assess the overall business objectives and to incorporate them into achievable deliverables. The *strategic services director* works with the account director in the early stages of the project. Through a series of client meetings, the strategic services director develops a needs assessment, which will become the foundation of the technical specifications.

If the project also requires targeted marketing, a *marketing or promotional manager* may also be assigned to the project. He or she will develop the marketing plan including cross-promotional strategies, the advertising plan, and e-mail campaigns.

A *researcher* may also be assigned to the project as part of the strategic services team. The researcher may assess competitive sites to deliver a focused positioning strategy.

Core Team

Although a project team may include dozens of talented individuals, it is the core team that will have the most significant impact on the quality of the final deliverable. This core team includes the *account director,* the *art director,* and the *interactive director* and may also include the *strategic services director.* A member's experience should include five-plus years in his or her chosen field of expertise (noting that the mass-market growth of the Internet has occurred within this time frame, parallel industry experience may also be appropriate) and may also include an advanced degree and a well-defined track record of projects.

Each core team member should be recognized in the vendor references, with notation of length of the affiliation with the vendor.

If the core team member is also an officer of the firm, this will be indicative of the firm's natural strength. For example, if the interactive director is also president of the firm, the company may naturally excel at technical solutions.

PROJECT TEAM

A typical project team will include the skills of at least five subteams: (1) project management, liaison between the client and the vendor team and responsible for the on time, on budget launch; (2) design team, responsible for the overall look and feel and corporate branding of the site; (3) development team, responsible for integration of system-level applications; (4) production, responsible for integrating the development and design services into a functional online experience; and (5) strategic services, responsible for marketing and focusing on the delivery of the overall business objectives.

■ VENDOR RESOURCES

Find out how the vendors position themselves in the industry by inquiring who they consider to be their key competition. Compare this to the previously developed internal list to both confirm and validate the vendor's positioning in the industry. Find out if it has any strengths (or weaknesses) in any particular system applications.

➤ Familiarity with System Applications

Does the vendor prefer off-the-shelf solutions, or does it attack each new project by building customized solutions? There is no right answer to this question. The effectiveness of the solution must simply be measured against the short-term goals versus long-term goals.

In parallel to its strengths, with third-party systems, consider the company's legacy systems and how it may impact the development of the web site. Be as explicit as possible not only about the scope and the configuration of legacy systems but also about the expectations of who will be responsible for integrating the web front end with the legacy back end.

➤ Training and Maintenance

Consider also the training and ongoing maintenance required of a full-time (24/7) web site. At the end of the project, will the vendor hand over a virtual key and walk away, or will the vendor be available day and night to address ongoing concerns?

Training can also be a complicated component of the project deliverable. Is the expectation that the deliverable will be a turnkey solution that can be maintained by non-technical staff or a bare-bones solution that will be fully supported by the internal web team?

➤ Project Scope

"Project creep" is also a major casualty of complex projects, which is why it is critical to set project objectives up front and to remain focused on them throughout the project. The objective may be as simple as a deadline—"We need to have this site go live by September 30 because this is the start of the sales season." Or it may be based on site functionality—

"We need an end-to-end transaction solution that will cut our product delivery time by 20 percent." Regardless of the objective, it is critical to the success of the project that the Internet manager is up-front with the vendor about the project goals. By vesting the vendor team in the project vision early in the process, the Internet team will be able to use their expertise to the project's greatest advantage.

➤ References

It would be very unusual (and counterproductive) for a vendor to provide references that were not glowing. To make the background check easier (and to be able to draw quick comparisons between vendors), request a standardized checklist about the references.

- ➤ *Project scope.* Ask the vendor to provide a brief description of the initial project and the final deliverable. Make sure that the objectives and the deliverables are generally consistent with the new project needs.
- ➤ *Team.* Find out the makeup of the team assigned to the project. If possible, find out if anyone from the proposed team worked on any of the reference projects. For a large company, this may be nearly impossible; but, at minimum, the references should provide enough information to be able to compare the typical experiences of a project team.
- ➤ *Time frame and/or budget.* A three-week turnaround may be commendable but inappropriate to the pending project needs, just as a $750,000 deliverable may not be relevant to the pending project scope. Inquire about the timing of the reference project. If the vendor is citing projects that are more than two years old (unless there is a particularly relevant industry

application), find out what they've completed most recently and why they are not using these projects as references.

➤ *Results.* Because hindsight is 20/20, when contacting references, find out if they have been pleased with the results since the launch. Have they hired the vendor for follow-on work? If they could do it over again, what would they change?

Reference checks should be a positive experience, confirming expectations of the vendor capabilities. They should be given willingly and received well. It is the simplest way to confirm the capabilities of a vendor.

➤ Project Management Skills

The vendor should be able to provide a concise description of how it manages projects. Find out about the ongoing responsibilities of the project manager. Will he or she provide a weekly update of project status? What are the vendor's expectations from the client side?

Communication is also a key factor in the success of any project. How often are meetings planned? Are deliverables online, or is there a formal presentation-and-review process? Both the client and the vendor team should set reasonable expectations up front for timing on the review-and-approval process. If the internal decision-making process required layers of approval, this should be shared with the vendor up front. In turn, the project management team should be flexible in their ability to respond to requests from different levels. Inevitably, there will be unexpected delays due to unforeseen circumstances. It should be clear up front how they will be managed and what impact they may have on timing and/or budget.

As the project unfolds, the scope may change. To prevent delays and cost overruns when the project is underway, policies and procedures about change orders (client requests for changes beyond the original project scope) should be carefully reviewed before the project begins.

■ VENDOR SELECTION

Finally, when selecting a vendor, carefully consider its size as compared to the project deliverables. Bigger is not necessarily better, but the Internet manager does want to make sure that the project is not sapping all the resources of the vendor to complete the project. At the same time, be sensitive to the fact that a small project for a larger vendor may be relegated to the junior B team as the A team focuses on more extensive projects.

At the end of the process, the Internet manager should have a final list of two or three vendors who should be able to deliver a successful web site. Chart their strengths and weaknesses and present them to other team members for review. Was each vendor generally receptive to all requests? Did the vendor respond to each request in a timely manner? Did he or she show genuine commitment to the project? A final visit to the vendor's offices will also provide some key clues about the vendor's professional character and capabilities.

DEVELOPMENT TEAM

A team may consist of a single vendor, or it may consist of multiple vendors. It is critically important to complete all levels of due diligence when selecting a vendor. This due diligence should include assessment of prior projects, reference checks with former clients, and presentations by the actual team members who will be responsible for delivery of the services as outlined.

VENDER SELECTION

In the identification of resources, the solicitation and selection of the development team should include a methodical analysis of potential vendors validated by a detailed due diligence. The development team may be part of one company, or it may include several distinct skill sets, such as a design shop or a technology firm. In summary, the key steps to selecting the vendor that can deliver on the objectives outlined in the project blueprint include:

1. Developing a short list of potential vendors.

2. Assessing the skills based on prior experience, company history, and individual skill sets.

3. Qualifying the service requirements from any one team or multiple teams, depending on the resources needed.

4. Mapping the critical team resources, and comparing them to the services offered by each vendor.

5. Analyzing the process deliverables in the context of the vendor portfolio as well as the individual project needs.

6. Completing a detailed due diligence.

7. Selecting the vendor team(s) that best meet the requirements outlined in the project blueprint.

Chapter 10

Finalizing the Directions

With the identification of resources, the final step in the project development process is implementation—the actual development, delivery, and ongoing management of the guidelines as outlined. There are three stages in the implementation process: (1) definition of the project time line, (2) delivery of project milestones, and (3) an ongoing assessment of project flow and the ongoing management responsibilities to ensure that the site achieves the underlying business objectives.

BLUEPRINT

The final section of the project blueprint includes the project schedule, which may be dependent on industry seasonality or corporate business objectives; reference to key contacts (may also include contact information for key internal personnel in areas such as information technology [IT] and marketing); and any predetermined budget preferences (such as total available resources or preferred fee structure).

To ensure the on time, on budget launch of the online strategy, it is critical to set development deliverables up front. These deliverables include a project schedule with finite milestones; definition of what is included in the initial development and what is included as part of the ongoing management; an up-front agreement on ongoing training and maintenance, ownership, and usage rights of the deliverables; and, finally, budget/cost parameters.

■ SCHEDULE

Can a site truly be launched in 90 days? It all depends on the scope of the project and the proposed objectives. In fact, a site can be launched in as little as eight hours:

Hour One—Find an Internet service provider (ISP) who provides web site hosting services and sign up for the service.

Hour Two—Open a word processing program, and create a few paragraphs of content for the site page.

Hour Three—Using existing clip art or dropping in some scanned photos, incorporate geographical elements into the page.

Hour Four—Take a break for lunch.

Hour Five—Save the created document in a format that is viewable by a browser, generally hypertext markup language (HTML).

Hours Six and Seven—Call the ISP for instructions on how to upload the file on the Internet server.

Hour Eight—Call friends and colleagues and give them the web site address.

Of course, the effectiveness of a site that is launched in eight hours is rather questionable although it can be done.

Launching a web site is not hard. Creating an online experience that will both drive the target audience to the site and cause them to act (whether that is buying a product, using online support, or sharing information) is the first challenge. The second challenge is launching a site built on tomorrow's technology because today's technology is already obsolete.

Why 90 days? Because the traditional business cycle is typically represented in 90 days and because, organizationally, 90 days present enough time for a team to gel and deliver. A 90-day schedule forces the Internet manager to target present deliverables without losing focus on the future; 90 days also assumes that there is already corporate buy-in and that the teams (both internal and external) have been generally defined as a result of detailed project guidelines defined in the project blueprint. And, of course, 90 days does not include the ongoing maintenance and administration that will be required to keep the site captivating. So, can a site be launched in 90 days? Absolutely. Should it be launched in 90 days? That depends on the situation.

The schedule of a 90-day launch goes something like this:

Week	Deliverable
1	Finalization of project plan
2	Contracting of vendor team
3	Development of site schema
4, 5	Production of content architecture
6	Design of site concept
7	Delivery and review of site alpha
8–10	Development of site beta

Week	Deliverable
11	Delivery and review of site beta
12	Final revisions and quality assurance testing
Launch!	Launch!

BLUEPRINT

The project schedule should include clearly defined milestones based on the business objectives and market conditions defined in the project blueprint. These milestones may include: a concept schema, a site schema, functional specifications, content architecture, design concept, alpha review, development, beta review, revision(s) and quality assurance testing, and launch. Post-launch, a finitely detailed maintenance strategy should then be executed.

■ PROJECT MILESTONES

Deliverables are driven by resources. A small team can provide focus but may lack the experience to deliver broad-scale functionality. A large team can deliver functional depth but may compromise the project time line. The reality of the implementation schedule is based on the following *milestones:*

➤ Concept schema

➤ Site schema

➤ Functional specifications

➤ Content architecture

➤ Design concept

➤ Alpha review

➤ Development

➤ Beta review and quality assurance testing

➤ Launch

➤ Site management

While these milestones are laid out in a linear path, many of the functions can run in parallel to one another. For example, although development follows review and sign-off of the site alpha, in fact, with tightly defined specifications, development can sometimes begin in parallel with the creation of the concept schema. As with any project plan, these milestones are to serve as guidelines and not inflexible delivery parameters.

➤ Concept Schema

Traditional print content is generally laid out in a linear pattern. For example, an annual report would provide background information on a publicly traded company. The experience is linear—one section would follow another. Although the reader could skip certain sections, it was nearly impossible to directly associate one topic with another unless there was a specific reference. In contrast, by embedding links into a web page, visitors can jump to specific topics of interest. For example, the annual report for General Motors is available through the investor information section of its corporate web site. The 1999 annual report begins with a short multimedia presentation highlighting the objectives and opportunities for General Motors and then provides a linked index to the main sections of the annual report (including financial highlights, letter to stockholders, financials, board of directors, and corporate information). When the user goes to the financial highlights section and rolls over a major category like "net sales and revenues," a small window pops up with a graphical representation of the three-year history of that specific category. Through the use of multimedia links and subpages, reviewing the annual report for General Motors is no longer a linear process but one that is built around specific user interests.

To initially create this experience, however, someone had to map out the information flow or concept schema that dictated the general guidelines for the user experience on the web site. In another example, a concept schema for a retail transaction site may consist of five user experiences:

1. Find product
2. Select product
3. Complete transaction
4. Receive confirmation
5. Return to site for another purchase
1. Find product . . .

A site concept schema is shown in Figure 10.1.

CONCEPT SCHEMA

The first milestone in the project plan is the delivery of a concept schema or site flowchart that defines the user experience that will most likely cause the anticipated business objective.

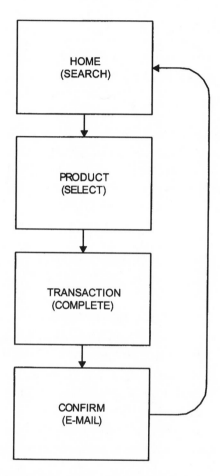

Figure 10.1 Site concept schema.

A concept schema succinctly defines the user experience that will most likely cause the anticipated business objective. It should be very straightforward and easy to understand. It is a graphic representation of the strategic statement and will form the foundation of the site schema. The concept schema may be developed by the internal team, or it may be created by the strategic services group.

➤ Site Schema

The site schema flushes out the actual user experience with all the bells and whistles. It will define pages that are static content (they do not change without editing the copy) versus those that are dynamically created (perhaps to show customer-specific information) versus those that capture information (through a form) or create some other action. Returning to the retail transaction model outlined earlier, the site schema can become quite complicated as the details of the user experience are finitely defined.

For example, the homepage may need to provide more than a search function. It may also provide a link to additional company information, contact information, recent press, and investor relations. It may also feature product specials as well as a log-in for previous buyers so that they can circumvent the tedious transaction process or rapidly reorder prior purchases. Thus, the initial concept box may expand to something like the site schema in Figure 10.2.

A working example of a site schema is the Wal-Mart web site. From the homepage of the site, the user can access corporate information in "About Wal-Mart," can search for products based on specific categories or through a product search, and can use a log-in for previous buyers.

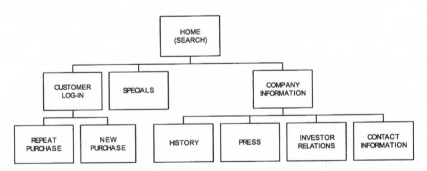

Figure 10.2 User architecture.

Selecting the product may include the ability to list selections by different criteria, such as price or manufacturer. It may also include external links to product reviews.

At each step of the process, the options become more complex as the user experience is further defined. That experience must be created through some sort of functionality. Returning once again to the homepage, each box may be further marked with a specific type of functionality. For example, the homepage may be modified and posted by an administrator (tedious but effective). The search function may run on a specific search engine that is tied into an inventory database. Further, there is some flag generated when a product is out-of-stock so that the search engine does not return it as a search result. Similarly, there may be some automatic trigger to feature products as "specials" when there is excess inventory or when a product is not selling as quickly as anticipated.

Corporate information may also be generated by an administrator, although it will need to further define how that content will be published. For example, will the administrator use a series of template specifically created to update the content? Alternatively, will the content be created to allow easy updates through an HTML editor like FrontPage? Or will the administrator be required to become an expert in HTML to update the pages?

Questions ranging from administration to functionality will be defined on the site schema as it is further detailed in Figure 10.3.

SITE SCHEMA

The site schema defines the actual functionality and process flow that will be embedded in the site and becomes part of the technical specifications.

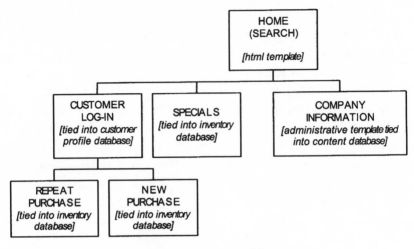

Figure 10.3 Process architecture.

As the site schema evolves, it becomes part of the technical specifications for the site. The site schema should be developed by the strategic services group in conjunction with the development and production teams.

➤ Functional Specifications

The site schema will help to define the front end of the functional specifications for the site. Previously defined in the technical specifications and used as part of the vendor selection process, the functional specifications will define the specific input/output features of the site. For example, the technical specifications may have defined an inventory database of 10,000 products to be accessed simultaneously by up to 500,000 people per day. Each product may have a series of up to 10 independent fields that may be combined to deliver certain search results. Reports quantifying the current status of the inventory may be generated via a complementary intranet site accessible only to the internal team. As noted earlier, it might also create "feature" items for sale based on slow-moving inventory or could permit the pairing of like products for group purchases.

By formalizing the user experience via the site schema, the functional specifications solidify the usability of the site schema. These functional specifications are created by the development team.

FUNCTIONAL SPECIFICATIONS

The functional specifications define the technical processes that will deliver the core features of the site and are typically created by the development team.

➤ Content Architecture

Although the functional specifications define the front end of the technical specifications, the content architecture is the actual mock-up of the site built on static content pages. Returning to the previous retail example, the homepage may include a series of links and a few paragraphs of information. The project page may include a sample search result with links to optional searches. The corporate section may also include static pages of content representing the anticipated user experience.

As a mock-up of the site, the content architecture will visually define the user experience—including navigation, page flow, and prototype functions. It can then be tested against the strategic statement. Using the retail model outlined earlier, the content architecture for the mock-up of the homepage may look something like Figure 10.4.

Figure 10.4 Content layout.

The purpose of the prototype is to finitely define the user experience and to prevent dead ends (click-through patterns in the site that lead to a page without access to the rest of the site). For example, to validate a company's experience and capability in selling products online, a user may click from the homepage to "about the company" to find out more about the company background. From there, the user may go to the online press room to find out if there have been favorable reviews about the company. After clicking on a few reviews, the user is ready to purchase a product from the company. But, in drilling down further and further into the site, the original "buy" button on the homepage has disappeared, creating a dead end and frustrating the ready, willing, and able buyer.

The content architecture addresses this oversight by defining both the content and the navigational elements on each page. Using the content architecture as a bare-bones mock-up of the site both prevents the development of dead ends and positions the various subsections of the site so that the linking relationships to one another are optimally designed.

This prototype also solidifies the primary and secondary navigational elements that will appear on every page of the site. *Primary navigational elements* are those links or calls to action that will appear on every page of the site (for example, "buy now"). *Secondary* (and even tertiary) *links* may be unique only to that specific section of a site (for example, "press releases" may appear only in the corporate subsection of the site). By defining these primary elements during the content architecture phase, the groundwork will be complete for the design concept. Both the production team and the design team will develop the content architecture. Again, the primary purpose of the content architecture is to optimize the user experience and to finitely define the site content structure to enable rapid development, launch, and management of the site.

CONTENT ARCHITECTURE

Developed by the production and the design teams, the content architecture will finitely define the site content structure and enable the rapid development, launch, and management of the site.

➤ Design Concept

The design concept phase draws on both the content architecture previously defined and the legacy corporate branding and identity previously outlined as part of the project blueprint.

At this stage, the design team incorporates these various elements into the first cut of the overall look and feel for the site. Depending on the time frame for this phase, the design team may develop a single design concept to present for review and modification or a series of design concepts, with one or two being selected for additional refinement. The initial deliverable may be just the homepage, with the addition of template designs for the secondary sections as the homepage is finalized.

Approval of the design concepts will then lead to the development of the site alpha.

DESIGN CONCEPTS

Developed by the design team, the design concepts will incorporate the existing corporate identity into an intuitive online interface.

➤ Alpha Review

Development of the alpha will include not only the design team but also the production and the development teams. A specific section or site functionality will be designated as the deliverable for the site alpha, and work will commence from there. In the case of the retail site developed earlier, alpha may include the production of the corporate section or, perhaps more effectively, the development of the customer profiling system in which previous orders are tracked and available for review by the customer.

Site alpha will be the first time that the project team will be able to test a functioning section of the site. It will also deliver enough functionality to demonstrate the business objectives of the online strategy to the target audience for the first time through a series of focus groups. Feedback from these focus groups is a critical part of the alpha stage. Focus groups should be used to test the intuitive nature of the proposed design, the efficiency of the information and navigation through the site, and the overall functionality delivered during the alpha phase. By incorporating focus groups into this early phase of the project, costly mistakes can be avoided at later phases.

With review and feedback from both the internal project team and the focus groups, full-scale development of the project can begin.

SITE ALPHA

With full coordination of the development team, site alpha will provide a working demonstration of a specific subsection of the site. It is the first critical stage, when all the pieces of the site strategy, from the business objectives to the development deliverables, come together.

➤ Development

This phase of the project will have the most expensive daily run rate, or cost, because it will incorporate the most team members. Depending on the scope of the project, this phase may incorporate both the internal and the external IT teams. It will draw heavily on the design team as they develop the interface for the functional components as delivered by the IT team. Finally, large-scale production will be underway as content is finalized and incorporated into the site.

Again, this phase may be very broad, encompassing weeks of development by the diverse teams; or it may be deep, as teams work closely with one another to turn around the project in a very short time frame.

Project management is absolutely critical at this stage because it is only the careful coordination of these many talents that will ensure that the project is delivered in a timely fashion.

And, with the successful completion of the development phase, the project is delivered in a beta state for final review and feedback.

DEVELOPMENT

This stage, the most expensive because it draws on the greatest number of simultaneous resources, is the actual building of the site to meet the specifications outlined in the project blueprint.

➤ Beta Review and Quality Assurance Testing

At this phase, the project has finally come together, and the initial vision of the management team begins to be realized. The site is launched on an interim staging server so that it can be tested for functional soundness (quality assurance testing). Ideally, it will also be reviewed by target-user focus groups. Finally, the senior management team should review the site to make sure that it realizes the initial vision behind the project blueprint.

This phase will require the longest review stage because the feedback from so many different groups is key. As the last stage before launch, it is the final opportunity to rid the site of anything ranging from technical glitches to user oversights.

Of course, along with review is the final fine-tuning of the site as every member of the team incorporates final changes prior to launch.

BETA REVIEW AND QUALITY ASSURANCE TESTING

The final beta review and quality assurance testing phase is the last opportunity for all users to test the site prior to launch. It should be functionally complete, pending minor changes and adjustments to meet the underlying business objectives.

➤ Launch!

Whether a *soft launch* (with little fanfare but public access) or a *hard launch* (which is announced with as much promotion as the budget allows), launch is the point when the site goes live and is the true test of the business objectives.

Of course, launch is just one moment in time. Now, the real work of marketing, management, and administration begins because the site has become a viable business entity.

■ SITE MANAGEMENT

Chapter 12 will provide more details about the ongoing management plan. In summary, however, it will include marketing, maintenance, and administration.

➤ Marketing

Marketing will begin by developing customer awareness through promotional programs, both online (banner advertising, e-mail programs, and cross-links) and offline (television, radio, direct mail, and public relations events). Once awareness is created and people begin to visit the site, effective marketing will ensure that the needs of the customer are met. Whether that is through the satisfactory delivery of a product or a timely reminder of a reorder, sustaining and maintaining customer needs, marketing will then be responsible for developing new programs to draw in new customers as well as to encourage existing offline customers to take advantage of the site's benefits.

➤ Maintenance

Maintenance will fall primarily under the jurisdiction of the technical team and will include the ongoing functionality of the site as customers needs change and the user base grows. It will also include responsibility in the area of security and client confidentiality as the data about each customer continues to evolve.

➤ Administration

Administration includes the daily updates and modifications to the site content. Whether posted automatically or inputted directly to retain the appeal of the site, it will be the responsibility of the administrative team to update it on a daily basis.

Each project milestone is predicated on the timely and efficient delivery of every other phase. Whether the time frame is eight hours or 90 days, the successful launch of a site depends on the timely delivery of these milestones.

LAUNCH

Launch is only a short milestone in the realization of the project objectives outlined in the site blueprint. Once the site "goes live," the actual work of meeting the business objectives begins. The site management phase includes ongoing maintenance, marketing, and administration strategies.

Once these milestones are achieved, the ongoing needs of the site evolve, and the management of the site may require ongoing maintenance agreements.

Ongoing Maintenance Agreements

As more strategies are valued based on customer relationships and information about individual customer habits, many companies are choosing to outsource much of their technical infrastructure. Because everything from the servers to the source code may be owned by another company, tight maintenance agreements are key to ensuring the ongoing success of the strategy.

Maintenance agreements should include backup policies, maintenance response, dedication of key staff, and ownership of customer information. Because this information may reside on a third-party server, these details are a critical part of the site management plan.

Ownership and Usage Rights

While it is satisfying to know that the inventory turn-over rate is decreasing, for example, due to this new distribution channel, it may be disconcerting to realize that it is impossible to track who is buying the products because all of this information is maintained on a third-party database that is inaccessible because of the development agreement.

Ownership and usage rights, still an emerging field, are a key component to the ongoing viability of the site. Who will administer the site? Who has access to content? What type of reporting methodologies are in place? All of these questions will need to be addressed as ownership evolves from bricks-and-mortar inventories to customer relationships and the unique ability to manage these relationships through unique customer information.

How easy is it to switch vendors if the maintenance is not satisfactory? What rights does the original vendor retain at this point? These possible scenarios should be addressed as part of the initial selection process and not left until after the project is completed because the ownership and subsequent value of this information will have a fundamental impact on project cost.

■ BUDGET AND COST PARAMETERS

Time, deliverables, and cost are the primary variables that define the delivery of a project. With an infinite budget, deliverables will more likely be achieved in a more timely fashion. However, few project managers will have an infinite budget, which is why it is critical to define the budget up front.

A budget will include both the internal soft costs of allocating internal resources to the launch of the site and the hard costs of the vendor contracts. The broader the team, the more costly the project management costs will be. Conversely, outsourcing the project to a single vendor may be costly because it will then be carrying the operational over-head of many different in-house resources.

Rather than building the budget based on outside vari-ables, begin by basing the budget on project objectives. For example, if the objective is to increase gross revenue by 10 percent, what are the current operational costs and what are realistic investments versus expenses? If the project plan is a trade-off of existing costs, what are those costs and what is a reasonable investment?

Because the Internet is still evolving, an online project may become a hybrid of research and development (R&D) and short-term investments. While the customer relation-ships achieved online will hopefully positively impact the bottom line for years to come, the steps to achieve economic parity through the Internet are still evolving.

IMPLEMENTATION PROCESS

The final section of the project blueprint includes a project schedule with clearly defined milestones, the development of an ongoing maintenance programs, and the finalization of the project budget. The key steps in the implementation of the site development include:

1. Setting a realistic schedule, understanding that the project will evolve over time.

2. Managing the project milestones with appropri-ate review and feedback policies to ensure timely delivery.

3. Setting an ongoing management program with clearly defined roles and ownership rights.

4. Basing the budget on both deliverables and inter-nal trade-off costs.

Chapter 11

Selecting the Navigators

Once the definition of the project time line and core deliverables have been developed, the actual project development process can begin. This project flow is managed by the project manager, but it also requires access and availability of additional internal resources throughout the development process. Because this phase is the actual implementation of the site guidelines, it is included in the project blueprint as part of the definition of the internal team roles and responsibilities.

Just as the roles and responsibilities of the third-party vendors are critical to the launch of a site, delegating the appropriate in-house responsibilities is also important. For example, 50 percent of the marketing staff's time may be required over the development period to develop the site content. This may have an impact on the soft budget as well as on the overall project timing. Clear definition of these responsibilities up front will streamline the project going forward. Once these roles are defined, then a series of project planning tools will help to ensure the timely delivery of the development plan. The day-to-day responsibilities of the internal team are then defined to ensure seamless delivery of the project milestones.

> **BLUEPRINT**
>
> Seamless implementation of the project blueprint is contingent upon (1) clear definition of the roles and responsibilities of the internal team and (2) the use of a series of project management tools to facilitate the management process. As the individual responsibilities of the internal team will change over the implementation phase of the project, it is important to define their roles up front so that consideration may be made for preexisting commitments.

■ INTERNAL TEAM

The key members of the internal team (see Figure 11.1) will be the project manager, the marketing coordinator, and the systems integrator.

➤ The Project Manager

The *project manager* will be the primary liaison with the external team, in many ways, a mirror image of the vendor team. The project manager will most likely report to the senior-level executive management team, which will include representatives from finance, operations, and strategy. Each of the senior team managers may then have a group reporting to them who are responsible for various facets of the project.

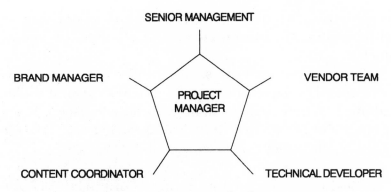

Figure 11.1   Core Internet development team.

In a high-turnaround project, in which delivery is assumed in a time period of no more than 90 days, competence in the various disciplines is key, but compassion, respect, and the ability of the team to gel in high-pressure situations will drive the ultimate success of the project.

The project manager is critical to the success of the plan. That person may be a corporate visionary, willing to stake his or her career on the launch of the project, or a former .com entrepreneur, recently brought into the corporate fold as the result of a merger or an acquisition.

In a 90 day launch program, the project manager should plan to devote anywhere from 50 to 100 percent of his or her time on the project. To put it plainly, there will be little or no other time for other projects. It is the responsibility of the project manager to launch this project on time and on budget. This will include juggling and prioritizing other people's schedules, inspiring the internal team, negotiating with the external team as the project scope evolves (and it will), and always remaining faithful to the strategic vision of the executive team. Secrets to success? Organization, patience, and flexibility. Motivating factor? An on time, on budget launch.

Before the project begins, the project manager should be well versed in the online space in which the project will be positioned. To the extent possible, the project manager should put himself or herself into the role of the target user. Like the target user, the project manager should:

1. Begin with a search of keywords in some of the top search engines and directories.

2. Check the results, but also note who bought the banner ads to those keywords.

3. Find out who has registered those keywords as domain addresses (unsophisticated end users may type in those keywords in the hope of finding information about the relevant topic).

4. Go back to the competitive list developed earlier and visit the sites.

5. Create a mental checklist of the number of clicks that it takes to get to the key information.

6. Go through the site as a novice user. Is it easy to navigate? Is the content current? What is publicly available, and what do you need to submit to access private information? Is the experience standardized or is it highly customized?

With all this in mind, the project manager should come to a cohesive conclusion as to what can be done to make the site better.

Of course, this is easy if the competition is online and is one keystroke away from dissection. But what if the competition is behind a firewall? Then the real homework begins. Check out the trade publications. Reference research groups.

With these details ready to present to the internal team, the project manager should begin to assemble the ace team that's going to get the job done.

➤ The Marketing Coordinator

Keeper of the brand, the *marketing coordinator* will defend the legacy of the corporate image while setting the standard to deliver an evolutionary relationship with the target user.

The marketing coordinator may also be responsible for drawing together a group of disparate brands that are traditionally marketed and promoted independent of one another and unify them under a corporate web site, while simultaneously forming the infrastructure to leverage the individual benefits.

For example, assume that the company is a group of automotive dealerships. Each dealership markets under a unique identity, but all report to a parent company. After detailed customer research, it is decided that the company will post near-real-time display of actual inventory at each site. Because each dealership is responsible for a different manufacturer, for internal competitive purposes, each dealer will only post cars appropriate to the dealership on the individual site. At the same time, to remain competitive with sites like Auto-by-Tel or Cars.com, which consolidate different cars on one site, the parent corporation will post an all-inclusive inventory with each lead distributed to the appropriate dealership.

Now, it is up to the marketing coordinator to make sure that the corporate image and that of each individual dealership remains consistent with the branded image. Whereas the systems integrator may be responsible for the back-end distribution of the appropriate inventory information to each of the sites, it is up to the marketing coordinator to develop and deliver a strategy in which each of the dealers knows how to respond both online and offline to the leads generated. Each dealer may want to publish "Deals of the Week." It will be up to the marketing coordinator to determine how this content should be developed and delivered through each web site.

In effect, while the marketing coordinator will be defending the historic legacy of the identity, he or she will also be setting the standard for the future of the brand in the online marketplace. His or her role must be forward thinking, not focused only on the user experience at the initial launch but also on how the online identity will evolve going forward.

Just as the marketing coordinator looks forward, it will be the responsibility of the systems integrator to look back to the legacy systems and to decide whether it is more effective to seamlessly incorporate them into the online strategy or to build parallel or even new systems to drive the engine of the online presence.

➤ The Systems Integrator

As a distribution channel, the Internet has the power to impact the core of any company's traditional business operations. For example, suppose the online strategy is to provide an online bill-payment system for an electric company. Then delivering real-time account information through a web interface simultaneously to thousands (if not more) users and then allowing those same users, with a click of a button, to forward payments into the company's coffers will most likely stretch the technical infrastructure of even the most innovative corporation.

It is the responsibility of the systems integrator first to decide what is feasible to bridge into the legacy system, then to assess the necessary steps, and finally to make a recommendation that will not cripple the system architecture.

In the case of online bill-payment for the electric company, a bill-processing system is already in place. Each electronic bill payment, like its print predecessors, can be processed the same way. Bills are batched and inputted into the system. This may require retraining of the staff to input these payment forms, but the input of data into the system remains the same. Eventually, this system may become inefficient, but it solves the immediate need of payment processing. An independent system may then be used to process the actual online transaction.

Drawing information out of the system may be a more complicated endeavor for the legacy architecture. Individual account information in the form of secure web pages will need to be created and produced in near real-time. Again, although the existing system may have been developed to allow internal review of this information, now this information will be accessible to thousands (if not more) individuals simultaneously calling in from disparate systems. A short-term solution may be to publish information that is updated on a delayed basis.

It is the role of the systems integrator to assess the short-term versus long-term system objectives to deliver the most efficient real-time experience. Unlike the marketing coordinator, who must look to the future user experience, it is up to the systems integrator to remain focused on the real-time user experience.

Together, the project manager who looks first to the outside market conditions, the marketing coordinator who

---

INTERNAL DEVELOPMENT TEAM

The core members of the internal development team are typically the project manager, the marketing coordinator, and the systems integrator. Together, they help to make sure that the project is launched on time and on budget.

must anticipate the future user experience, and the systems integrator who remains focused on the real-time experience form the core internal team (with critical support) to ensure the on-time, on-budget process of launch.

■ PROCESS FLOW TOOLS

For the life of the project launch phase, each of the core members of the internal development team should be prepared to devote the majority of their time to the project. However, while each of these managers will lead the initiatives outlined in the project plan, the delivery of the site will require varying time commitments from a diverse support team using a predefined set of management tools.

Although the project manager will be focused on the overall plan objectives, he or she will also be responsible for managing the day-to-day deliverables of both the internal and the external teams.

Because of the compressed time frame of the project, an online project plan, accessible by all team members, will help to manage everyone's expectations. Each third-party vendor may develop an online project plan specific to his or her deliverables, but that plan won't reflect the internal team deliverable. An online project plan is a valuable tool in the seamless implementation of the project blueprint. This project plan should include the following elements:

> ➤ Team Directory. This directory will include a list of all team members, including their contact information (e-mail and phone number) and their role in the project. Anyone who has worked on a round-the-clock (24/7) project will appreciate the one-click, late-night access to a team member, even though the response may not be generated until the next day.

➤ Project Schedule. Because of the critical importance of launching on time, this project schedule will allow everyone to remain focused on the deliverables. A slip in one part of the project might impact another deliverable, so this online schedule allows every member of the team to track progress and to modify deliverables. For example, while the internal team is developing site content, the external team may be creating a series of design concepts. On approval of the design concepts, production of a series of page templates can begin. However, because of a delay in the internal copywriting process, delivery of the content is extended another week. Rather than halting design development entirely (creating idle resources), the design team may be able to recommend a staged delivery of the content. This staged delivery will then allow the designers to continue work in parallel with additional content development. The project schedule optimizes flexibility while enabling the project to remain on track.

➤ Deliverables. While the project schedule will manage the horizontal development of the project, a detailed description of the project deliverables will set defined expectations for the vertical delivery of the project elements.

In the case of an online retail system, the delivery of Internet-based transactions may include a customer profiling system integrated into the existing customer database, arrangements with a merchant bank to allow the transfer of funds, agreements with the major credit card companies to accept their credit cards, and integration into a product fulfillment system. Each of these tasks fall under the deliverable of "e-commerce enabled" but will most likely require an in-sync combination of internal and external resources. As a vertical plan, the project deliverables provide the detailed depth of tasks and responsibilities enabling the project to launch on time.

➤ Milestones. The fourth element of the online project plan is the delivery of the various project milestones that will be linked to the milestone list. In this way, each team member has immediately available access and can adjust individual responsibilities accordingly.

While these tools will better enable the project manager to manage the launch process, he or she may also enlist the assistance of a producer who can help alleviate bottlenecks (such as delays in the internal review process) as they occur. The producer will also help to call in additional resources that may be needed and can track the project budget on a weekly basis.

MANAGEMENT TOOLS

Management tools to ensure the on-time, on-budget delivery of the project guidelines include a secure resource site with the following information: team directory, project schedule, defined deliverables, and project milestones.

■ TEAM RESPONSIBILITIES

The primary role of the project manager, assisted by the producer, is to ensure that the project stays on path for an on time, on budget launch. However, the roles and responsibilities of the marketing team and the IT team will evolve as the project progresses. They, in turn, will call on other internal resources to deliver specific expertise during the implementation phase.

➤ Marketing

The *marketing coordinator* is responsible for meeting the overall marketing objectives. Working to support these objectives will be individual product managers.

The *product managers* will help to define the optimal online experience for their target audience and will be involved in both the very early stages of the process and the later stages when the site is in beta review. In the early stages, the marketing coordinator should meet with each of the marketing managers and should coordinate both existing resources and anticipated deliverables. As exemplified earlier, the marketing manager will then be responsible for organizing these resources in an online experience that delivers the appropriate individual message in a unified format. This process will often include the distinct needs addressed by the manager of corporate communications.

Once these deliverable are defined, the role of the marketing coordinator will then shift to managing the delivery of the internal resources. An internal copywriter may be assigned to integrate the various communications messages of the individual product managers. This content may be published in a word processing format that will then be delivered to the external team for incorporation into the web site. Again, this process will occur in the relatively early stages of the plan.

The marketing coordinator will also be responsible for delivering the branded visual elements of the site. These elements may include product photos and logos, as well as any specific design specifications in regard to typeface or color palette. The marketing coordinator may also work with a graphic designer to deliver any missing internal elements. In certain cases, the marketing coordinator may work with the internal audio or video specialists to deliver branded corporate elements in these various fields. Once again, the organization and delivery of these projects will occur rather early in the project process.

On delivery of the various elements, the role of the marketing coordinator will shift to a supervisory role, and he or she will be responsible for ensuring the integrity of the marketing message online.

➤ IT Team

Depending on the technical depth of the project, the systems integrator will work with a team that includes engineers, application developers, and network administrators to ensure the seamless transition into the online marketplace.

The systems integrator will play a critical role in the early stage of the process as the various system requirements are defined. He or she will be instrumental in defining realistic challenges to integrating the online systems into legacy applications and may also guide the critical decision to integrate or migrate. This decision may not be made, however, without the critical input of his or her support team.

Does the corporation have enough bandwidth to administer and maintain the site in-house? What are the pros and cons of outsourcing the site servers to a third party? Network administration will play a critical role in making these decisions.

What about ownership of the source code? How many off-the-shelf applications will be incorporated into the site development versus customized development that the corporation will own? Who then is responsible for ongoing administration, maintenance, and modification of these applications if they are built to spec? The internal application development team, whose lives may be made miserable with the wrong decision, should have a strong say in this strategy.

Customized development versus prepackaged solutions will also have an impact on the budget and time line. Owning the source code may create a competitive advantage but a financial nightmare. The information technology (IT) team must address these issues as they apply to the specific deliverables.

Finally, ongoing support will have a fundamental impact on the success of the site. Once the switch is flipped, who is responsible for making sure that the light stays on? What about upgrades or revisions to the original application? Without careful development of a maintenance plan by the IT team, postlaunch may prove to be an IT nightmare. Culling from the best internal resources, the systems integrator can develop a clearly defined implementation plan that is well suited to future upgrades.

In this way, the original team of three lead managers expands into an internal network of corporate professionals. Recognizing that these professionals, whose day-to-day priorities will most likely not be driven by the site launch, the following time line provides a brief outline of critical responsibilities at each stage of the project process.

MANAGEMENT TEAM

After defining the various responsibilities of each team member, his or her individual contributions can then be matched against the various project milestones.

■ INTERNAL TEAM RESPONSIBILITIES WITHIN THE PROJECT PROCESS

➤ Concept Schema

Core Responsibility: Project Manager

As the strategic statement evolves to define the user experience, the project manager should be focused on working with the senior management team to ensure the implementation of the anticipated deliverables. The concept schema will then be reviewed by the marketing coordinator and the IT manager to ensure that the anticipated deliverables are achievable.

➤ Site Schema

Core Responsibility: Marketing Coordinator

The site schema will define the actual content flow-through within the site. At this stage, the marketing coordinator will work closely with the product managers to address the needs of the individual target audience. With these needs quantified, the infrastructure of the site is set.

➤ Functional Specifications

Core Responsibility: Systems Integrator

To ensure the real-time delivery of the planned user experience, the systems integrator will step in at this stage to define the core functionality and the architecture of the site. These specifications will include both integration into the legacy system and development of the independent system architecture. With the internal functional specifications defined, the technical architecture can be set.

➤ Content Architecture

Core Responsibility: Marketing Coordinator

The marketing coordinator will then oversee the delivery of the content for the site. Working closely with the product managers and copywriters, he or she will provide the content that will define the user experience.

➤ Design Concepts

Core Responsibility: Marketing Coordinator

The branding of the site now begins with the marketing coordinator defining the internal design specifications and any layout requirements for the site.

➤ Alpha and Review

Core Responsibility: Project Manager

The external team will then begin to develop the site prototype that generally includes the site homepage and several subpage templates as well as limited functionality. The project manager will work with the external team to ensure timely delivery and review of the site alpha. The alpha may then be used for focus group feedback.

➤ Development

Core Responsibility: Project Manager

With feedback and approval of the site alpha, the external team can then begin full-scale work on site development. The project manager plays a general, overseeing role at this stage, ensuring that the external team meets the project deadlines.

➤ Beta and Review

Core Responsibilities: Project Manager, Marketing Coordinator, Systems Integrator

Like the alpha process, the project manager now leads the review of the beta site that should include all content and site functionality. The beta will also most likely be presented to the senior management team for review and approval. This stage will be the critical point for review prior to site launch and should also include review and approval by the marketing coordinator and IT manager.

➤ Revision and Launch!

Core Responsibility: Project Manager

As the project nears launch, it is the responsibility of the project manager to ensure that all the pieces have fallen into place and that the site meets the core business objectives.

➤ Maintenance and Administration

Core Responsibility: Project Manager

Depending on the ongoing responsibilities of the project manager, the project manager may continue to manage the ongoing administration of the site or may turn it over to the site administrator.

MANAGEMENT ROLES

The responsibilities of the internal team will evolve throughout the project flow. Defining roles and expectations up front will facilitate the overall implementation strategy.

PROJECT MANAGEMENT

Implementation of the project plan requires the careful coordination of an entire team lead by a project manager, a marketing coordinator, and a systems integrator. The project manager should orchestrate the implementation program through a series of online project management tools, while each team coordinator may be responsible for working with other internal resources at specific stages of the site development. In summary, the key steps in managing the implementation process internally include:

1. Assigning motivated individuals to manager the core responsibilities of project management, marketing, and systems integration.

2. Creating an online tool kit including a team directory, a project schedule, and deliverable and milestone lists.

3. Defining the support team and ensuring that their input is incorporated into the overall project process.

4. Defining the core responsibilities of the team leaders throughout the project process.

Part IV
Implementation

Chapter 12

Navigating the Launch

It's happened! After months of hard work gelling a vision through the experienced hands of an Internet team, the site is launched. Unlike the grand finale at the end of a star-studded performance, the launch is like the maiden voyage of a beautiful ship—the real work has only just begun. There are significant long-term challenges to meet the business objectives outlined in the project blueprint. The next step is the actual realization of those project milestones so carefully defined at the beginning of the project planning process.

This final chapter therefore returns full circle to the beginning of the project blueprint where the initial business objectives were outlined and can now be implemented. To assess the achievement of these objectives requires careful management, administration, and measurement of online results.

The objective of the project blueprint is to provide the guidelines to launch a site on time and on budget. After the launch, the blueprint process begins over again with the development of a series of guidelines to enable the seamless management and administration of the site. This operational blueprint is driven not by strategic objectives but by specific operational objectives that define the day-to-day

BLUEPRINT

Launch is only the first step in the realization of the on-line business objectives. Only effective ongoing management, administration, and measurement strategies will guarantee the success of the ongoing business strategy. The final step in the launch strategy is the assessment of the project blueprint as the beginning of the development of a new set of guidelines, the operational blueprint.

responsibilities inherent in the management of a site. The following strategies define the transfer of the site from the development stage to the operational stage. These strategies include the reassignment of the management team and the definition of the ongoing administrative strategies in conjunction with management of user expectations. At the end of this stage, a new project management plan, the operational blueprint, is developed to meet the objectives of the ongoing business strategies.

■ FROM MANAGEMENT TEAM TO OPERATIONAL TEAM

The team, which broadened considerably with the development of the site, will now be pared back to reflect the core competencies of sustaining the site functionality. The *Internet manager* will remain in place to oversee the day-to-day execution of the site strategy. A *content administrator,* or site editor, should be assigned, along with a support team, to ensure that the site content remains fresh and relevant to audience needs. A *customer support administrator* (an often overlooked responsibility) should serve as the conduit between addressing evolving customer demands through the site and addressing them through traditional offline communication channels. For example, a spike in telephone support calls as a result of unanticipated ambiguity about the site would be funneled through the customer support administrator and adjusted through a site change. A *site designer* should also be included to work hand in hand with the site editor to maintain the cognitive expectations of the end users. Finally, a *systems integrator* should be included in the core management team to ensure the ongoing execution of the site functionality. This may include retained management by application service providers (ASPs), who maintain the integration between the legacy systems and the Internet architecture. The management should then evolve as shown in Figure 12.1.

Each team leader will then manage the appropriate support team as relevant.

■ LAUNCH

After months of hard work, the site is finally opened to its target audience. Companies will approach the launch stage differently depending on the breadth and the scope of this audience. For example, a major consumer-driven strategy that is predicated on attracting thousands of users may include advertising, promotion, and public relations programs to ensure maximum impact with consumers. A site targeting

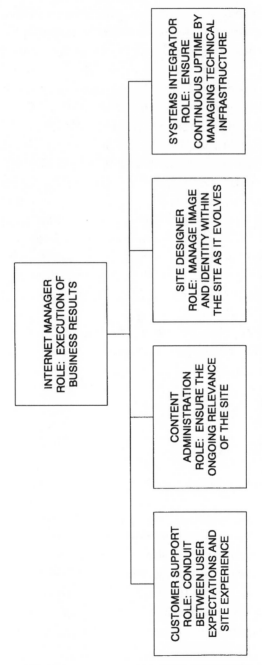

Figure 12.1   Internet management team.

a discrete group of vendors may launch with a phone call or an e-mail to each participant. Regardless of the size and the scope of the target audience, the launch is the critical juncture when it is determined if expectations will be met or if the site fails to meet the immediate goals.

Expectations for the site will range from design to content to functionality. Is the experience intuitive? Do visitors drill down beyond the first page? What is the most popular section of the site? Well-executed design will create the intuitive user experience. Content, and its continual updating, will ensure that users will return to the site. Finally, site functionality will be put to the test with ongoing site traffic.

SITE VISITS

If the site has been correctly positioned in its market space, initial traffic to the site will be the first indication of success. If the traffic increases or there is a noticeable number of repeat visitors, then the site has viability. If the target users interact with the site, whether that is through registrations, transaction or other online mechanisms, then habits have been redefined and the site has begun to generate quantitative results, meeting the goals set by the project blueprint.

■ ADMINISTRATION

Administration of the site should include not only the daily maintenance of site content and user expectations but also a regular program to assess the macro issues of positioning, competition, and user experience.

➤ Customer Support

The relationship with the end user that was carefully analyzed prior to site launch should now be reflected in the day-to-day usage of the site. For example, are the day-to-day customer support strategies consistent with the real-time needs of the end user? Tracking of customer support programs may include access of the frequently asked questions (FAQs) section of the site, e-mail requests and response, or instant online support and callback systems.

The Adobe web site, for example, delivers a strong example of the implementation of extensive user support strategies. Titled "CustomerFirst," customer support strategies include "Top Issues," which is a list of answers to the most frequently asked customer support questions. Updated monthly, the FAQs are regularly updated to respond to the most relevant customer inquiries. Through CustomerFirst, users can also search a database specifically addressing answers to product questions. Downloads of latest software updates are also included as part of CustomerFirst Support. Technical Guides are detailed documentation that provide technical specifications and troubleshooting guidelines. Adobe also supports user-to-user forums, allowing users to interact directly with one another. This level of interaction also provides Adobe with direct access to user solutions and helps the company to address evolving user needs. Adobe's support system also provides the capability for users to sign up to receive e-mail updates about the latest technical announcements, taking a proactive rather than solely reactive position on using e-mail to manage customer support. There is also a series of direct customer support programs, as well as access to a third-party support service. Finally, Adobe directly asks for user feedback through their satisfaction survey. Adobe is one example of a company that actively creates an ongoing online support strategy to meet the needs of the target user.

➤ Site Maintenance

If the objective of the site is to create an ongoing incentive for repeat visitors, then the information on the site must be updated on a regular basis. CNN.com provides continual news feeds. However, there has to be an administrative process to parse the data into the online format. This requires the commitment of a team of content administrators who are part of the ongoing operational staff. Depending on the overall business objectives of the site, there needs to be an operational team in place to address the ongoing management of the site.

■ OPERATIONS

Unlike the project blueprint, which specifically details the strategies and the processes to enable a successful launch, the operational blueprint outlines the ongoing management responsibilities to ensure that the site meets its overall business objectives.

As the site falls into a day-to-day routine, the tracking of business results begins. If the objective of the site is to shift a parts-procurement process online, how many users visit the site in the initial weeks of the launch? How many of them then commit to stage two, which may be to request a request for proposal (RFP)? Does the number of qualified vendors increase as a result of the online procurement process? By monitoring the results in the early stages, the online strategy can be modified as appropriate.

Operations also include the ongoing analysis of market conditions. Are the expectations of the target audience shifting? Have new competitors launched since the initial analysis? Have existing competitors shifted their strategies based on this site launch? Again, a steady schedule of assessing the online landscape should be included as part of the execution phase of the management plan.

Another critical part of the operations stage is the transfer of technical administration. While an application service provider may be managing the ongoing applications, there will most likely be an internal team, lead by the systems integrator, who will manage the internal modifications to the core information databases. For example, while transactions may be executed through the application of a third-party system, the existing inventory system may be managed internally. The ASP might deliver ongoing support of the internal system. Unless it is defined up front, documentation may not be part of the ongoing administrative deliverables. Similarly, site training may or may not be included. It is therefore critical to outline these maintenance deliverables at the outset of the project.

Representations and warranties in regard to capacity and uptime should also be defined during the planning stages. System failure during execution could have a detrimental impact on site usage.

■ AFTER THE LAUNCH

The operational blueprint is created based on the realization of specific business milestones and the evolution of existing market conditions. Like the project blueprint, the operational blueprint will also include a definition of business objectives, assessment of market conditions, and assignment of resources.

Thus, the process begins once again. The Internet manager brings results back to the senior management team who review it and develop a general consensus for the next objectives and deliverable results. These objectives may be based on the results of the current Internet strategy. For example, if the strategy attracted 10,000 committed users, what are the next steps to attract 100,000 users?

The strategy may also be to launch an entirely new program. If the first launch was to decrease supply chain costs, the second launch may target an entirely new audience and focus on delivering product to a new market base. These disparate strategies may require the support and development of a new team while leveraging the experience of the first team. However, now there is a process in place to organize the next launch.

The Internet manager then reviews the objectives with the now seasoned internal Internet team to develop a set of new site specifications. These functional specifications are then revised to become the RFP. The RFP is solicited to a select group of vendors who then submit a proposal. The proposal is reviewed for scope, and the third-party vendor team is selected. Technical specifications are written and approved. Development work begins and goes through a highly iterative approval process. With final deliverable, the new site is launched and operations begin once again.

SITE OPERATIONS

Launching a successful online strategy requires the cooperation of many diverse talents who all target a goal that is newly defined and subject to continual revision. With vision, team spirit, and patience, the Internet manager has the unique opportunity to set a precedent and to define a strategy.

(Continued)

(Continued)

With the launch of an online strategy, the site moves from development to operations. Operational strategies include:

1. Defining the skills required to support the ongoing site operations.

2. Developing an ongoing strategy to assess evolving market conditions.

3. Analyzing response through user feedback and interaction.

4. Developing an operational blueprint to implement new business strategies and to react to changing market conditions.

Appendix

Project Blueprint

The successful execution of an online strategy is contingent upon a well-executed project plan. The following outline serves as the guidelines or blueprint for the project plan.

SECTION 1: STRATEGIC STATEMENT

Define the industry:

_____

_____

_____

_____

Summarize the traditional business process:

_____

_____

_____

_____

Outline the online business process:

_____

_____

_____

Define the site efficiencies to be achieved:

_____

_____

_____

Define the business objectives:

_____

_____

_____

Define the metrics to measure the results:

_____

_____

_____

SECTION 2: MARKET CONDITIONS

Define the Target User

Create a process chart that defines the roles and responsibilities of the primary users:

_____

_____

_____

Summarize the demographic and psychographic profile of the target user:

_____

_____

_____

Define the technical profile of the target user:

_____

_____

_____

Create a Competitive Positioning Strategy

Prioritize the primary competitive variables:

_____

_____

_____

List both the horizontal and the vertical competitors:

_____

_____

_____

Summarize both the strengths and the weaknesses of the competition online:

_____

_____

_____

Create a competitive positioning chart:

_____

_____

_____

Summarize User Expectations

Define the value proposition:

_____

_____

_____

Target key marketing strategies:

_____

_____

_____

Develop a retention strategy:

_____

_____

_____

SECTION 3: DESIGN AND BRANDING

Define naming conventions and/or naming strategies:

_____

_____

_____

Define the existing corporate identity:

_____

_____

_____

   A. Logo:

_____

_____

_____

   B. Color Palette:

_____

_____

_____

   C. Typeface:

_____

_____

_____

Define and/or attach samples of offline marketing material:

_____

_____

_____

If coordinating efforts with an outside advertising agency, note contact information:

_____

_____

_____

SECTION 4: SYSTEM ARCHITECTURE

Define legacy systems:

_____

_____

_____

Define preferences for system infrastructure as appropriate:

_____

_____

_____

Define hosting and access strategies (include hardware specifications):

_____

_____

_____

Define internal resources and processes as they will impact web site development:

_____

_____

_____

Define firewall and security systems:

_____

_____

_____

Define ongoing maintenance requirements (include training):

_____

_____

_____

SECTION 5: VENDOR REQUIREMENTS (TO BE DEFINED BY VENDOR)

Project team:

_____

_____

_____

Project management process:

_____

_____

_____

Partnerships and alliances:

_____

_____

_____

Experience and capabilities:

_____

_____

_____

References:

_____

_____

_____

SECTION 6: TIME LINE AND BUDGET

Define project schedule:

_____

_____

_____

Outline internal team roles and responsibilities:

_____

_____

_____

Set budget criteria:

_____

_____

_____

Index